Macramé

BY BETSY MILAM

GROSSET
GOOD LIFE
BOOKS

PUBLISHERS · GROSSET & DUNLAP · NEW YORK
A FILMWAYS COMPANY

Acknowledgments

Cover photograph by Mort Engel.

Grateful thanks to the following people: my macramé class at the Bedford Hills Women's Correctional Facility for trying ideas for me, Jane Griner, Delcina Wilson Walker; Stefan Findel for his masterful photography; and lastly, my remarkably patient husband and family.

Contents

Introduction

Several years ago, a friend gave me a book on macramé and a word of advice: "Don't be afraid to try it; it's much easier than it looks." Though I've never been the kind of person who learns facilely from the printed page, I persevered. My friend was right. It was easy!

With only the first two knots covered in this book you can make many beautiful things, and the addition of a few more knots will make your knotting that much more interesting. The variety possible from simple combinations of knots appeals to the novice and serious craftsman alike. Both hands are used equally, so there is no problem for left-handers.

Hopefully, this book will inspire both the beginning knotter, who feels the need for a pattern to follow, and the more adventuresome, who want to explore further possibilities. The patterns have been selected to cover a broad range of objects. After learning the basic knots and making some of the projects included here, you will be able to "read" macramé pieces without written instructions or patterns. Macramé encourages creativity because it does not confine the craftsman to the problems involved with tools, blocking, sizing, fitting, etc.

So have a good time and don't be afraid to deviate from patterns that don't suit you. It's almost impossible to make a "mistake" in macramé because the saying "anything goes" really does apply here. A whole chapter has been devoted to new applications of fiber art, and some of these works will surely send your imagination soaring.

History of Macramé

There are no written records of the beginnings of macramé. However, since macramé requires no tools, it probably predates weaving by an enormous length of time, making it one of civilization's oldest arts.

The art of macramé as we know it evolved in the Middle East around the thirteenth century A.D. The Turkish word *makrama* (meaning napkin or towel) and the Arabic word *migrama* (meaning embroidered veil) were used to describe fringed pieces. The French word *macramé* was used to mean a kind of fringe on hand towels. During the fifteenth and sixteenth centuries the art of macramé spread to Italy and Spain, where pieces were used extensively in churches for religious items. In England, where it became popular during the seventeenth century, it was called *macrame lace*.

In the United States it was the sailors who brought "square knotting" to an artistic high point. The long hours at sea and the very limited materials forced a return to creativity that produced some of the most beautiful pieces of macramé ever done. The Seamen's Church Institute in New York City has some fine examples of this work, as do the Whaler's Museum at Mystic Seaport, Connecticut; the Smithsonian Institution in Washington, D.C.; and the South Street Seaport Museum in New York City.

Today macramé is an international pastime, having enjoyed a renaissance over the last two decades. Craftsmen, freed from the necessity of creating purely utilitarian objects, have found the freedom and variety of macramé a challenge and are exploring the ever-widening possibilities.

Facing page: A maserpiece of macramé, this massive frame is typical of the square knot practiced by American sailors in the nineteenth century. It contains over 11,500 knots. White cotton seine twine 39 by 43¼ inches. Collection of Seamen's Church institute, New York City. Photo: Stefan Findel

1
Materials for Knotting

The materials for macramé are very basic—a working surface, something to fasten the knotting to the surface, scissors, and cord. Your local hardware store, lumberyard, or craft shop should be able to supply you with everything you need for any project you have in mind. If you plan to work in color, unless you dye your own cord, the best supplier is probably a craft shop. Hardware stores usually have a good supply of cotton seine twine, jute, and nylon, but they very rarely have it in colors.

Your working surface can be anything capable of holding a pin and providing a surface sturdy enough to pull against. A clipboard, a piece of fiberboard, a foam slab, a padded brick, and an easel for long hangings all work well. A dress form is a functional support for clothing, as is a wig stand for headpieces.

Fasteners include T-pins, wig pins, pushpins (if the work is small), and upholstery pins. A C-clamp or two is handy for holding center cords of knotted sinnets (series of the same kind of knots tied into a braid) to the bottom of your working surface.

Knots can be made—and have been made—in every type of cord, yarn, rope, and string. Knots have even been made in some materials that seem strange to use, such as plastic bags, plant stems, and animal hair. However, some materials simply do not work as well as others for a given project. Materials that are too slippery to hold a knot or too lumpy to show off the shape of a knot are not worth the time invested. And some materials simply are not strong enough to withstand the tension of tying knots or to sustain hard wear. Select your material to suit the project you are planning.

Cords are classified as man-made and natural. Man-made cords include synthetics: nylon, polyethylene, polypropylene, and acrylic. There is a tremendous choice of color available, and the synthetics usually wear longer when it is necessary for them to be exposed to weather. However, they are almost always medium to high in cost. Natural materials consist of plant and animal fibers: jute, hemp, linen, sisal, cotton, raffia, manila, wool, and silk. Jute comes in a large number of sizes, is readily available, and is inexpensive; but it tends to shed when worked, and it does not have the durability needed for outdoor pieces. As a general rule, sisal is so rough and scratchy that it takes a dedicated knotter—wearing gloves—to use it. And silk, while lovely to look

A selection of macramé materials: wooden rings, cord, twine, bells, beads, a hoop, a piece of bone and wooden pegs.

at, is difficult to keep knotted and is best left to the experienced knotter.

Cotton seine twine, often called mason's chalk line or white line, is found in a larger variety of sizes than anything else and is easily dyeable, workable, and relatively inexpensive.

It is probably the best all-purpose cord for the beginner to use.

Braided cords are beautiful and give a different look to the finished work, but don't use them if you plan fringes or any unraveled ends. They are practically impossible to separate.

Some balls of cord are sold by weight and some by length. All should be clearly marked with the diameter of the twine. The ply has to do with the separate lengths which are twisted together to form a cord; it has nothing to do with size.

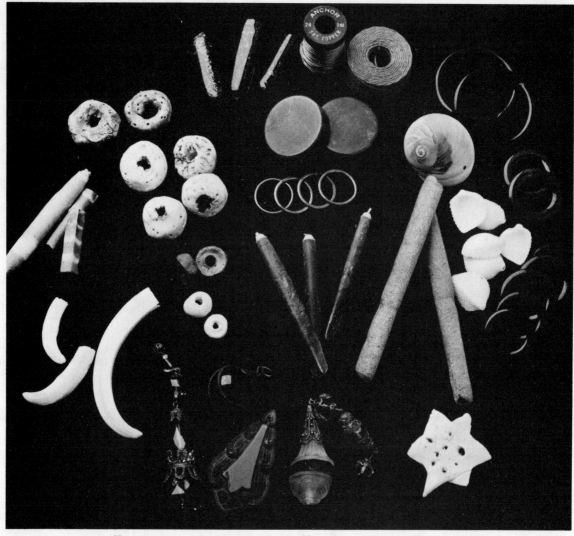

You can use your imagination in assembling your macramé material: anything from sea shells to polished stones and unusual pieces of jewelry.

Opposite: Norwegian Belt—circa 1920. Made of braided sinnets of square knots using cotton seine twine.

2
The Basic Knots

Half Hitch

The half hitch, or *macramé knot,* is the basic knot of macramé. It can be worked horizontally, vertically, or diagonally.

The illustration shows a horizontal half hitch made with two cords: the holding cord (A) carries the knots, and the tying cord (B) is used to make the knots.

The tying cord B is brought from behind the holding cord A, over and down to the left side. Pull it tight to form the half hitch. This knot will not stay secure unless there are at least two hitches over the holding cord (see Double Half Hitch, below).

REMEMBER: The holding cord always lies on *top* of the tying cord, and the tying cord always comes from *under* the holding cord. Also, keep the holding cord taut at all times; if it becomes slack, the knot will twist and must be retied.

Horizontal Double Half Hitch

The double half hitch consists of two half hitches tied in succession with the same tying cord. A series of double half hitches is called a *bar*.

This knot is indispensable to macramé so practice it, remembering to keep the holding cord *taut!* Like the half hitch, it can be tied either to the right or the left and should be practiced with both hands. When tying to the right, use your right hand for the holding cord and the left hand to tie with—reverse this for a left-hand knot. This may seem awkward at first, but you'll find it pays dividends when you're knotting a large project.

To tie a double half hitch, follow the directions for the half hitch. Then bring tying cord B up over holding cord A again. Next pull end B down through the loop you've just created. Pull tight to complete the knot.

REMEMBER: When knotting a bar directly below another bar, hold holding cord A diagonally *above* the previous bar to keep the knots tight against the previous row. The first half hitch places the knot and the second half hitch secures the knot.

Half Hitch

Horizontal Double Half Hitch

Double Half Hitch Row

Reversing Direction with Rows of Double Half Hitches

Vertical Double Half Hitch

The texture of your knotting changes dramatically when you reverse the holding cords and the tying cords. The vertical double half hitch allows you to continue a color across your knotting that would be hidden under cords with the horizontal double half hitch.

To tie a vertical double half hitch, use the horizontal cord as the tying cord. The vertical cord now becomes your holding cord. Remember to keep the holding cord on top of the tying cord. Make two half hitches for each knot. Pull down tight to complete the knot.

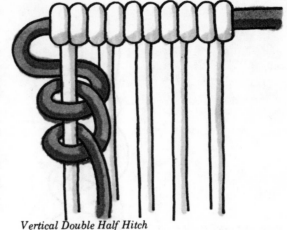

Vertical Double Half Hitch

Diagonal Double Half Hitch

Pin the holding cord at the angle you wish it to remain and tie onto it with the tying cords.

Collecting Knot

The collecting knot can be made using any number of cords. It can be made either from the right or from the left. Here it is shown from the left. The left-hand cord is used to tie a vertical double half hitch around a group of filler cords to the right of the tying cord. It can be used to form a pattern by dividing an even number of cords, tying with the far left-hand cord, then halving cords for the next row, etc.

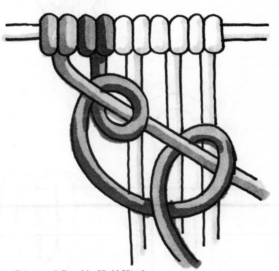

Diagonal Double Half Hitch

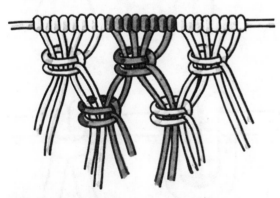

Collecting Knot Pattern

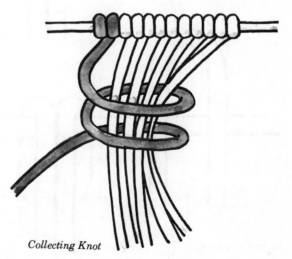

Collecting Knot

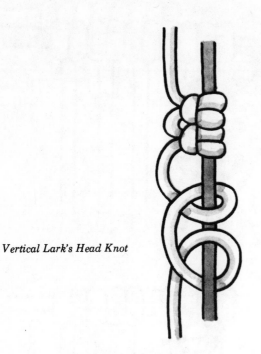

Vertical Lark's Head Knot

Lark's Head Knot

Used to begin a knotted piece or to add cords when shaping, the lark's head knot becomes self-explanatory when you refer to the illustrations. The cords are doubled and looped over a holding cord or bar. Then the ends are brought down through the loop. It can be tied from either side; choose the one which most appeals to you.

This knot also may be tied vertically with two cords or multiples of two. One cord is tied around the other, as in the illustration. The tying cord is first looped *over* the holding cord. Then it is looped *under* and pulled taut to complete the knot. Be aware before planning to use this knot that it uses a lot of cord, at least eight times the length of the holding cord to be covered.

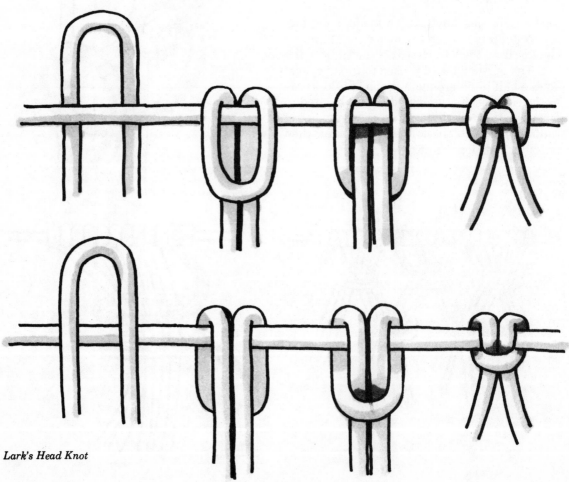

Lark's Head Knot

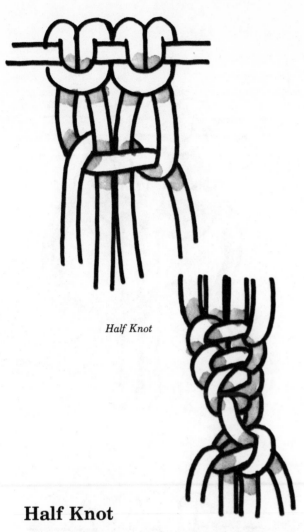

Half Knot

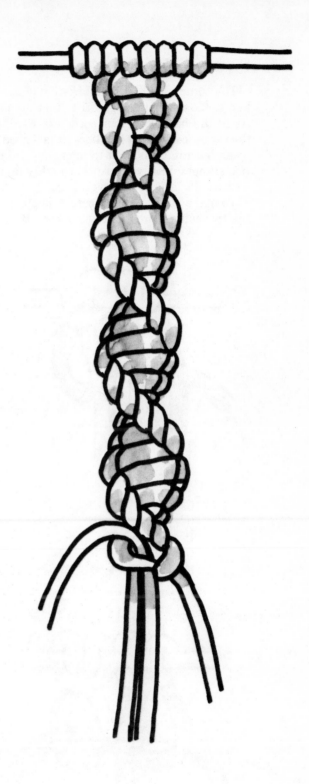

Half Knot

The half knot is made with four cords, two filler cords and two cords for knotting around the filler cords. Always hold the filler cords taut either by wrapping them around a C-clamp at the bottom of your knotting board or by pinning them to the board. The C-clamp method works better because it allows the filler cords to be raised slightly from the surface of the board, thus leaving working room for your fingers.

Spiral Knot

Notice after you have completed several half knots that the sinnet (braid) you have made is not lying flat but twisting to the right. Let it. Turn the sinnet over and continue knotting the same way to make a spiral.

Spiral Knot

Square Knot

The square knot is a combination of two half knots, one tied to the right, the other to the left. As in the half knot, four cords are used, with the center cords used as fillers. It is a good idea when learning this knot to make several practice sinnets until you are thoroughly familiar with all its variations. Several are shown here.

To make a square knot, cord A is placed *over* the two center cords and *under* cord B, etc.

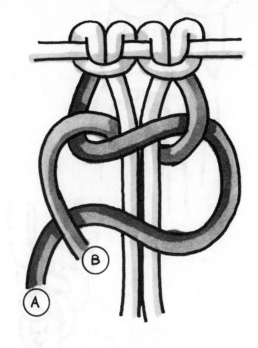

Square Knot

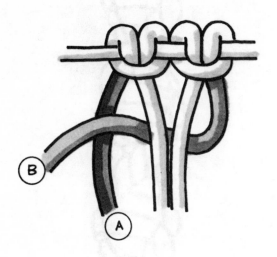

Square Knot

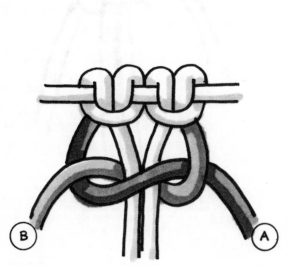

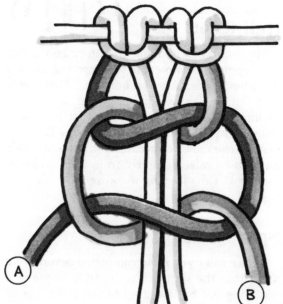

Alternate Method for Square Knot

This is a shortcut method for making sinnets of square knots. It is helpful only when your knotting is secured to a board or pad and the filler cords are pinned down. Although this technique looks complicated, give it a try. It will save lots of time for you when you've mastered it.

Start with two doubled cords. Pin the center filler cords down. Leave at least a foot of space between the knots and the pin to allow working room for your fingers.

Lay cord 1 in a U shape *over* filler cords 2 and 3. With your right hand, reach through the loop of cord 1 and under filler cords 2 and 3. Grasp both sides of the U made by cord 1.

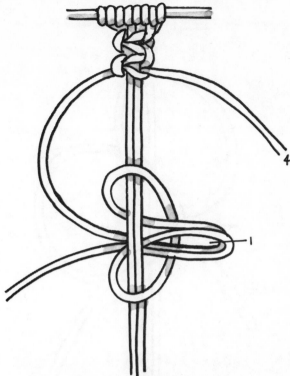

Alternating Method for Square Knot   Step 2

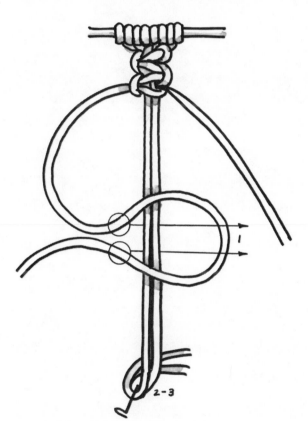

Alternating Method for Square Knot   Step 1

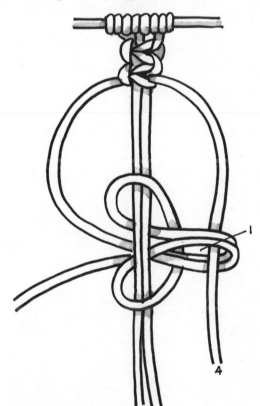

Alternating Method for Square Knot   Step 3

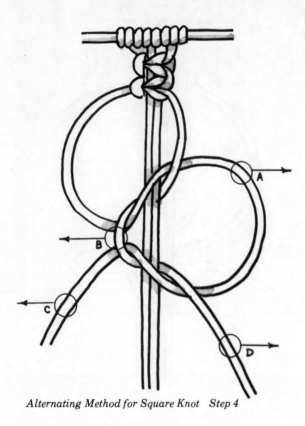

Alternating Method for Square Knot   Step 4

Pull this loop (loop 1) through to right of filler cords. Bring cord 4 down through loop 1.

With the cords in this position, pull cord 1 to the left and cord 4 to the right.

Your knot now looks like this. Pull it into final position as follows: Pull at point A to the right and at point B to the left at the same time. This ties your first half knot. Finish the square knot by pulling point C to the left and point D to the right simultaneously.

Opposite: Sampler by Betsy Milam.

3
Expanding Your Knowledge

Crown Knot

The crown knot is a very adaptable, useful knot to know. Tie it with two, four, or eight cords, or with any number at all. It is especially beautiful when tied with a great many cords, since it becomes massive and sculptural. The easiest way to learn to tie a crown knot is with a flat cord, so the shape of the knot becomes obvious right away.

There are four steps to follow:

Bring the left-hand part of cord A *over* and back to the left around the right-hand cord B.

Bring cord B up in *back* of cord A and straight down *over* cord A, leaving loop 1.

Then bring cord A *over* cord B and through loop 1. Tighten the knot carefully to keep the shape.

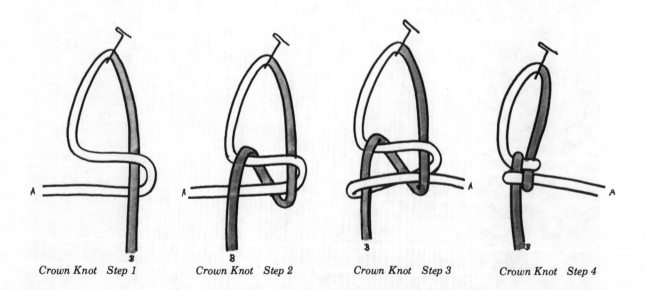

Crown Knot Step 1   Crown Knot Step 2   Crown Knot Step 3   Crown Knot Step 4

Crown Knot Sinnet

Instead of tying the crown knot horizontally as described above, the knots in this sinnet are tied vertically. This uses quite a lot of cord, so allow at least three times the finished length of cord for each group.

Hold the cords in the left hand, divided into 4 even groups. You can use any number of cords for each group.

* Take group 1 and lay it *over* the center of all the cords to the right, leaving *loop A*. Lay group 2 down *over* group 1. Lay group 3 to the left *over* group 2.

Then take group 4 and lay it *over* group 3 and *under* group 1, pulling it through loop A (made with group 1). Now tighten the knot by pulling all 4 groups down.

Repeat from * as many times as necessary.

Crown Knot Sinnet

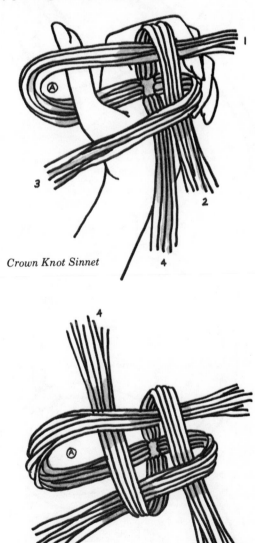

Crown Knot Sinnet

Crown Knot Sinnet

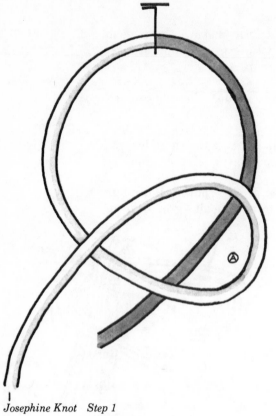

Josephine Knot   Step 1

Josephine Knot

The Josephine knot is a woven knot, or braid. Use it decoratively when the piece you're knotting doesn't have to take much strain, because when this knot comes under tension the shape tends to stretch out.

It is tied with two cords or multiples of two cords. You'll find it's prettier when tied with at least four cords, two for each side.

With cord 1, make loop A by going down, then to the right, and then back across the vertical cord.

Bring cord 2 diagonally *under* loop A and *over* the end of cord 2 at left. Put a T-pin in loop A to hold it in place.

Now you will start to weave cord 2 *under* vertical cord 1, *over* the top of loop A, *under* cord 2, and *over* the bottom of loop A.

Pull up cords 1 and 2 alternately and carefully to tighten this knot.

If you tie several Josephine knots in succession all starting from the left-hand cord (see illustrations), the knots will start to twist. If you want them to lie flat, tie one knot from the left and the next from the right. Reverse all directions shown.

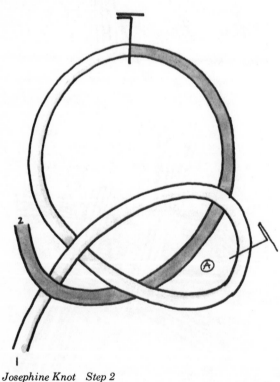

Josephine Knot   Step 2

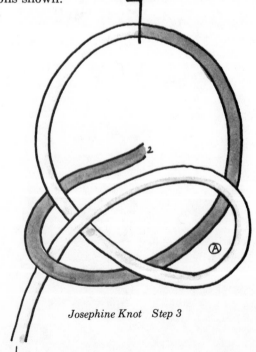

Josephine Knot   Step 3

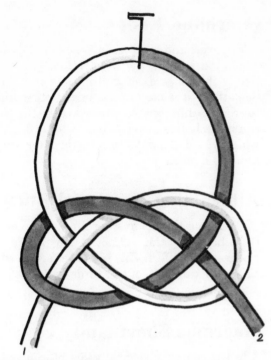

Josephine Knot Step 4

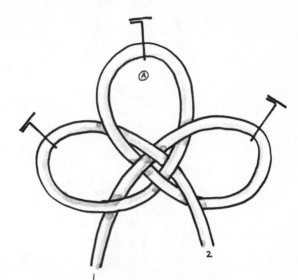

Turk's Head Knot Step 1

Turk's Head Knot

The Turk's head knot is a ring-shaped braid tied with one cord around a cylinder or a bead. It can also be laid flat to form a rosette. Two methods are used to tie this knot, and it's always best to use the method most suited to the occasion. Use the method shown here to tie a flat rosette, which makes a beautiful hot pad for the dining table, or tied with large rope, a door mat.

This knot was a favorite of sailors in the nineteenth century, and you can see some fine examples of it tied into the picture frame in the photograph on page 7.

Make a Josephine knot so that the loop made at the top by pinning (loop A) becomes part of the knot.

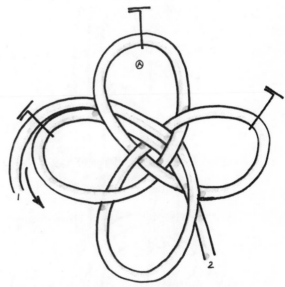

Turk's Head Knot Step 2

Bring cord 1 *over* cord 2. Then begin to weave cord 1 parallel to cord 2 around the knot. Repeat this weaving process as many times around the knot as you wish.

Overhand Knot

The overhand knot becomes self explanatory when you refer to the illustration. It may be tied with two cords or multiples of two cords. Sometimes it is used in a sinnet of other knots to create a different texture or to take the place of a bead. It also comes in handy to tie off ends, which you don't want to unravel after you've finished a piece.

Alternating Overhand Knot

Changing the holding cord from one cord to the other every time a knot is tied gives a decorative chain effect. This is most effective when tied with multiples of two cords (see *Headings*, page 27).

Macramé Shorthand

In the course of several years of knotting, I have developed a kind of shorthand for planning macramé pieces. It is fast, easy to do, and clearly "readable." Many of the illustrations in this book are drawn in this manner, so I'll familiarize you with it now:

Horizontal double half hitch ——∞——

Vertical double half hitch

Lark's head knot ——∽——

Spiral knot

Square knot

Sinnet of square knots

Crown knot

Overhand knot

Bead

Wrapping

Collecting knot

Josephine knot

Turk's Head knot

Alternating Overhand Knot

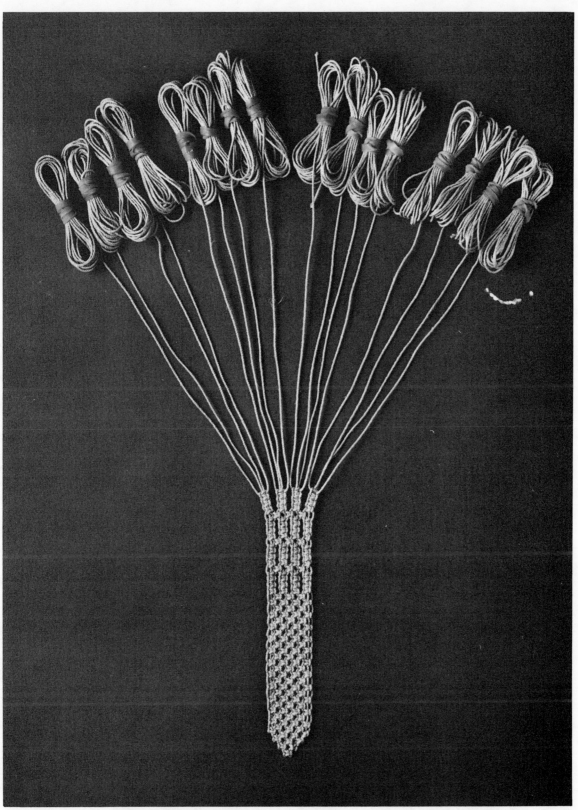

Working with long cords can be a nuisance. One way to avoid problems is to wind the cords and secure them with rubber bands. Always start about 2 feet below the working area and do not wind from the end of the cord (see page 29).

4
Working Methods

Planning

In knotting a piece of macramé, there are lots of things to consider. This chapter explains those that are necessary to you as a beginning knotter as simply as possible.

The first thing to do when you have planned a piece of knotting is to stop and think: Will it be worn? Will it be used outdoors? Will it hang by a window in the sun? All of these help determine what type of cord to use. If your project is to be worn (for example, a vest, necklace, or bracelet), then you should select a cord that is not scratchy and will become pliable with wear. Most new macramé pieces are rather stiff when knotted closely, but they become softer and more comfortable after a few wearings. By the way, macramé can be washed by hand, in warm water and a little detergent; it can even be scrubbed with a brush if necessary. Just rinse it well and spread it in the sun to dry.

Outdoors, moisture is fatal to jute within a couple of years, unless the jute is creosoted. Cotton also has a limited life span. Nylon is your best bet for outdoor plant hangers and furniture, since it is rotproof and moisture resistant.

Inside, when you want to hang a plant hanger or window screen where it will receive a good deal of sunlight, remember that dyed colors fade slightly and that the natural colors are more stable.

Once you've dealt with these considerations and chosen your materials, the next question is how to begin. Most beginners feel more comfortable with patterns to learn the knots. They begin to feel confident about the knotting and to see the different possibilities in macramé. After a while some begin designing their own pieces; while others undertake more involved patterns. Either way, you can have a lot of fun familiarizing yourself with the craft.

So it's time to start knotting. There are many different ways to begin. Some pieces are begun from a ring, others from a bar, still others from a cord that becomes a part of the finished project. Some circular pieces are begun from the center and expand outward, others from the outside and work in. You can attach your cords with a simple lark's head knot or get as fanciful as you wish with picots and headings.

Picots

Make a square knot. Then make another square knot about 1 inch below it. Push the second square knot up tightly against the first, forming loops, or "picots." You can make larger picots by increasing the distance between knots, or you can thread a bead on either the filler cords or each picot before tying the second square knot.

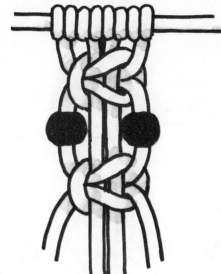

Picots

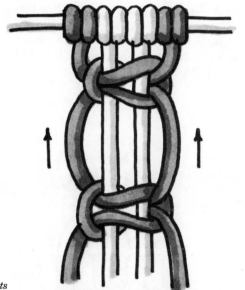

Picots

Headings

There are many different ways of starting a macramé project, depending on the use of the piece. If you are making a wall hanging, sampler, necklace, or other flat piece, you would usually start by tying your working cords onto another cord or support of some kind. Commonly the lark's head knot is used for such a beginning.

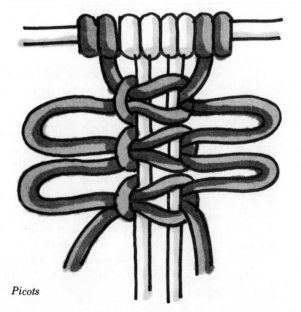

Picots

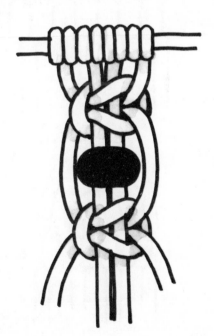

Picots

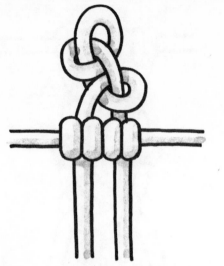

Headings 1

Here are a few variations on headings that offer more interest and variety to the beginning of a piece than the lark's head knot. They are knotted from either one or two cords.

Illustration 1 shows one cord that is tied in two alternating overhand knots before being double half hitched to the holding cord.

Illustration 2 shows two cords tied the same way.

Illustration 3 is a series of two picots double half hitched to the holding cord. You can add as many layers of picots to this heading as you wish.

Illustration 4 shows a square knot tied with two cords and then fastened to the holding cord with a double half hitch.

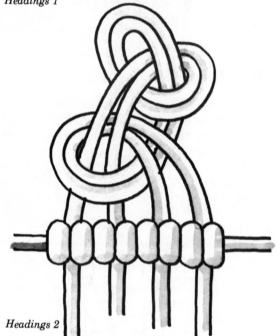
Headings 2

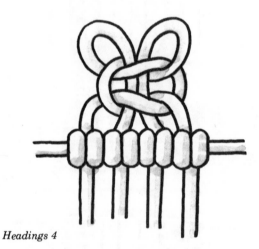
Headings 4

Starting from a Point

This method is used when you want to knot a belt, and there are several variations. Here are four of them, two with the cords tied onto a holding cord with a lark's head knot (see illustrations 1 & 2), another tied on with the double half hitch (see illustration 3), and another with no holding cord but with a pattern of alternating square knots (see illustration 4).

It is important to keep these patterns pinned to a board as you work, adding pins at the side knots of each new row.

Headings 3

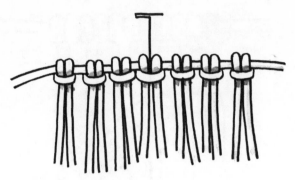

Starting from a Point 1

Starting from a Point 4

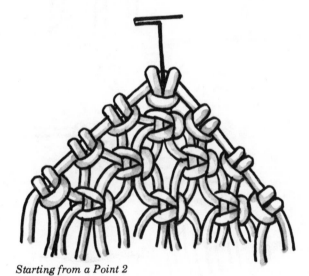

Starting from a Point 2

What to Do with Ends

When using cords that tend to ravel at the ends, such as jute or cotton, dip the ends in glue and twist the cords tightly. Or with large cords, seal the ends with masking tape.

With nylon cords, hold the ends close to a flame until they fuse. *Don't touch the ends until they've cooled!* They stay hot for about 30 seconds.

Bobbins

Long cords become tangled and get to be a general nuisance. There are several ways to handle this problem. Just remember to start winding cords from about 2 feet below the working area, *not* from the bottom (they won't unroll if you do). You can use rubber bands or another piece of cord to secure the cords. Or you can tie the end of the same cord around the bobbin with a double half hitch.

Starting from a Point 3

Replacing Cords

When you are using jute, sometimes you will unwind it to find a knot or frayed spot in the middle of a length you need. Don't worry, use it. Usually, the bad places work right into the knots and you can't tell they're there. Of course, if they happen to fall in the middle of a cord that's alone between knots, you'll have to substitute another cord in its place. For more about adding cords, see Shaping, page 33.

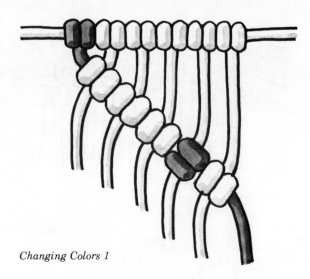

Changing Colors 1

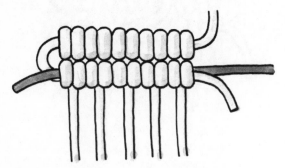

Replacing a Cord 1

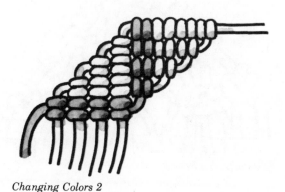

Changing Colors 2

Replacing a Cord 2

Changing Colors

If you are knotting a piece with the double half hitch, you can change the colors (see illustration) by using a contrasting cord to make a vertical double half hitch in a row of horizontal or diagonal double half hitches. The holding cord then becomes the tying cord for one or more knots.

This is an example of Cavandoli knotting. The Cavandoli pattern originated in Italy and was used to show school children how to create textiles with the color pattern made by the knots. Two knots are used, the horizontal and the vertical double half hitch.

Tying onto a Ring

The thing to keep in mind when tying any number of cords onto a ring (or any other form that is not a cord) is that the ring (or other form) is acting as a *holding cord,* and therefore should be held in *front* of your tying cord.

Illustration A shows the ring with the cords pulled through it to give stability. The upper portion of the ring is in front of the cords. Enough cords are used to cover only the upper half of the ring. Tie them onto the ring with the

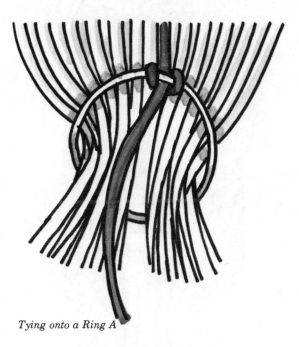

Tying onto a Ring A

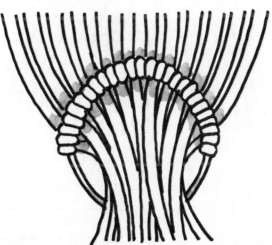

Tying onto a Ring B

Watchbands by Rikki Ripp. The larger of the two bands is a beautiful example of the Cavandoli pattern. The color is reversed on each side. Silk and nylon cords.

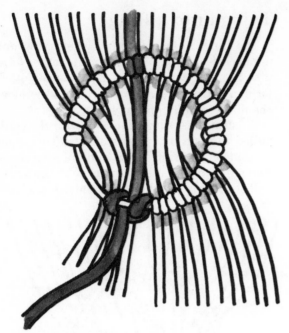

Tying onto a Ring C

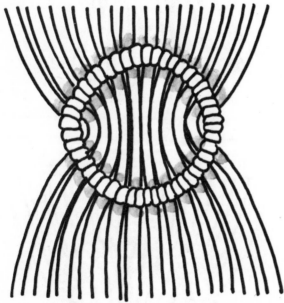

Tying onto a Ring D

double half hitch, starting with the top cords and working down to the sides alternately.

In illustration B, all the cords have been knotted onto the ring. The top half of the ring is completely covered, and the cords are still pul-

led through the ring to the front. Pull them back through to the back of the ring before you begin knotting on the remaining cords.

In illustration C, half of the cords have been knotted onto the remainder of the ring. To knot these on, you may start from the side cords and knot toward the bottom of the ring.

Illustration D shows the finished ring, covered with double half hitched cords.

Joining Edges

When you have knotted a three-dimensional piece, such as a handbag or vest, there are two basic methods for closing the seams so that they are invisible when the project is completed. If your project is square knotted, join a separate cord at the top of the seam and square knot it between all rows, looping the side cords of the square knot filler and the side cords of the rows together as the seam lengthens (see illustration). If you used the double half hitch in your project, weave a filler cord between the loops made by the holding cords of the hitches.

Another solution to this problem is to knot your project over a form. For a purse, the form could be a box, weighted for stability, or a filled bag the size you want the finished project to be. A dress form works satisfactorily either for vests or for elaborate necklaces that fit over the shoulders. In these instances, when you use a form, the entire piece may be knotted as a unit so that there are no side seams to worry about.

Joining Edges with Double Half Hitch

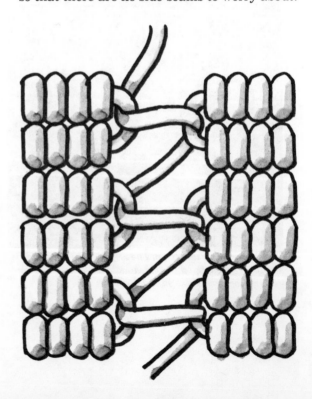

Shaping

Sometimes a piece of knotting should widen or narrow as it progresses, so you need to know how to add or subtract cords from your work. For instance, if you have knotted the top of a plant hanger and you want to add a ring to give the knotting shape as it progresses, then you have to add some cords to the ring to cover it. Or if you are making a flat object with a border, you may want to add cords to turn the corner. Several ways to do this are shown in the illustrations for adding new cords.

Just as you add cords to enlarge a piece, remove them when you have finished a section and they are no longer needed.

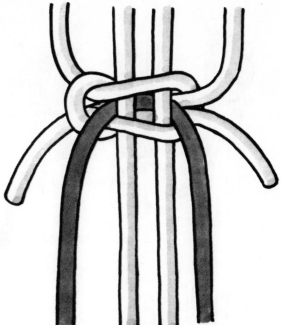

Adding a New Cord to Square Knot

Joining Edges with Square Knot

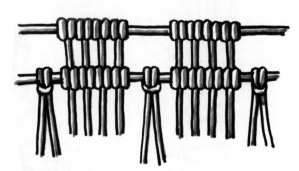

Adding New Cords to a Lark's Head Knot

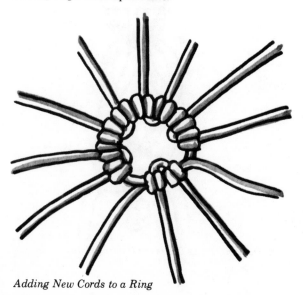

Adding New Cords to a Ring

Three-dimensional Knotting

Before you progress to this point, you ought to have a little experience behind you. The most commonly made mistakes when shaping a three-dimensional piece involve lack of planning and insufficient knowledge of adding and deleting cords.

While not difficult, the blue plant hanger project serves to start you thinking about what happens to a narrow-shaped project that widens suddenly. Knowledge of different methods of adding cords helps here and you can begin to branch out into coil work

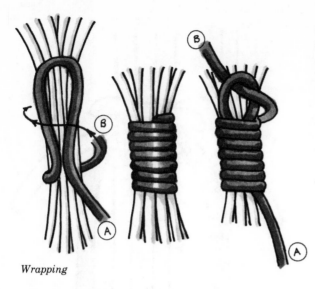

Wrapping

(coiled basketry is not only possible with macramé but also easier than you think) and intricately shaped pieces, such as hanging lamps and multi-leveled plant hangers.

Wrapping

Wrapping is a good way to make a tassel using scrap ends of cord you'd otherwise throw away. Save pieces over 2 feet long for this knot. The cords are first gathered together and secured with or without a rubber band, as you prefer. Begin the wrapping with end A held downward and forming a loop. Bring end B around and around the loop and the gathered cords, as tightly as possible, until the desired length of wrap has been achieved. Then bring end B through the loop and pull end A (pliers may be in order here) until the loop has disappeared under the wrap. Cut and glue both ends A and B and your wrapping is complete.

Sometimes you may want to do a long wrapping (over 6 inches). In this case it is impractical to tie with the loop method just shown. Instead, start the wrap with a very long tying cord and pull it tightly over end A as you wrap. Then continue wrapping until the desired length has been reached. Thread end B through a yarn needle and force it back under your wrapping. Pull the needle out and cut end B (see illustration).

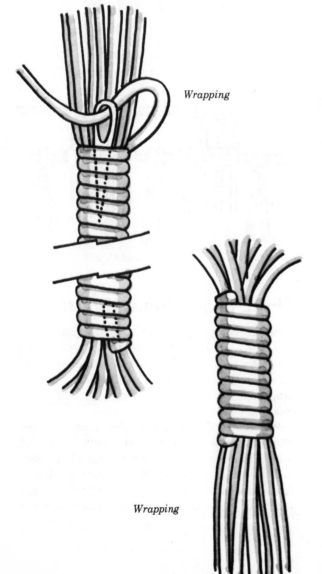

Wrapping

Wrapping

Exchanging Tying Cords for Holding Cords

Exchanging Cords

Sometimes when you are knotting a long sinnet of square knots, the tying cords begin to shorten quickly. If you see that you won't have enough length to finish, bring the tying cords into the middle of the knot and tie around them with the holding cords. This exchange of cords may be left loose (see illustration) and used as a design element in the knotting, or it may be tightened to become almost unnoticeable. You can repeat this variation at intervals to form a pattern in your knotting.

Finishing

What to do with edges? Depending on the object you have knotted and the considerations of use, style, and durability, a decision has to be made about ending it. There are many different ways of doing this. Some will be presented here; others you will discover on your own as you work.

Usually, macramé pieces are left to hang free on the ends, either unraveled or tied into bunches with tassels, or fringed in a more elaborate fashion. Sometimes, however, because of the use to which a particular piece will be put or simple preference on the art of the knotter, ends need to be finished so that the cords don't show. Several methods are possible:

Use a crochet hook to pull the ends through to the back, where they can be cut off and glued down.

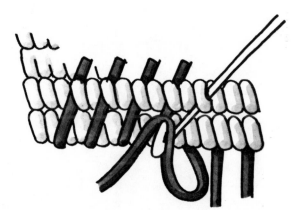

Bring the ends to the back, where they can be square knotted together, cut, and glued.

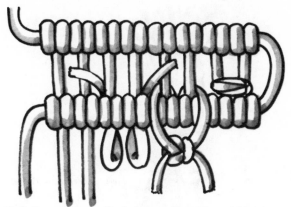

Ends Brought to the Back, Square Knotted, and Glued

Machine sew the ends to a tape, turn the tape to the back, and hand stitch it to the knotting.

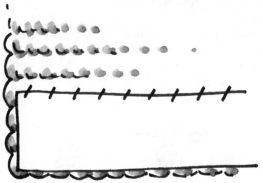

Ends Machine Sewed to a Tape

There are also several methods of making tassels.

Gather these cords together in bunches. Then square knot the outer cords around the inner ones.

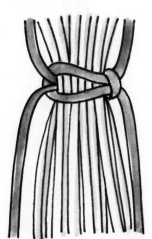

Tassel Cords Gathered in Bunches and Tied with a Square Knot

Tie a wrap around the groups of cords with a scrap cord.

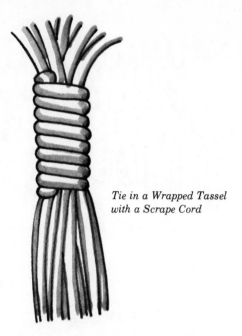

Tie in a Wrapped Tassel with a Scrape Cord

Tying extra cords onto one of the original cords will thicken a fringe that looks too skimpy.

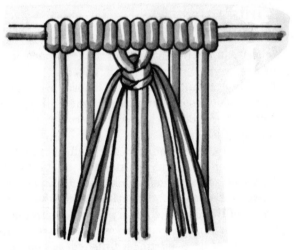

Thicken Fringe with Extra Cords

Twist each of two groups of cords to the right and combine the two groups by twisting them together to the left. Tie an overhand knot in the bottom to keep them from untwisting.

Bracelet on a Ring.

5
Projects

Bracelet on a Ring

This delicate bracelet is easy and fast to complete, and making it teaches you how to join cords onto the clasps necessary for jewelry. Some antique flat circular shapes are used, but the lark's head knot, which is used to join the cord to the circle, can be used with almost any shape. So you can adapt this pattern to a great variety of objects you may have on hand: beads, shells, small pieces of wood, glass, etc.

Materials
4 yards of 4-ply waxed linen, waxed nylon, or any hard twisted small cord (#12 approximately)
1 flat ring shape or anything you want to use
1 bracelet finding, consisting of 2 rings and 1 clasp
White glue

Step 1
Cut 4 lengths of cord, each 1 yard long. Fold them so that the loop is 6 inches from one end and 2½ feet from the other end. Knot them onto the ring with the lark's head knot. Arrange the knots as shown in illustration. You can fasten the piece to a clipboard at the ring or pin it to a board.

Step 2
Take the group of 4 cords from either side of the ring. Using the 2 longer outside cords, knot a sinnet of half knots, or a spiral knot, for about 2½ inches.

Step 3
Loop the inner 2 cords over the small ring of the bracelet finding and bend them back over the ring. Using the 2 outer cords, tie a square knot around the looped inner cords. Pull the knot tight and put a spot of glue on it. When it is dry, cut the ends off short next to the knots. Repeat from Step 2 for the other side, knotting onto the ring that holds the clasp.

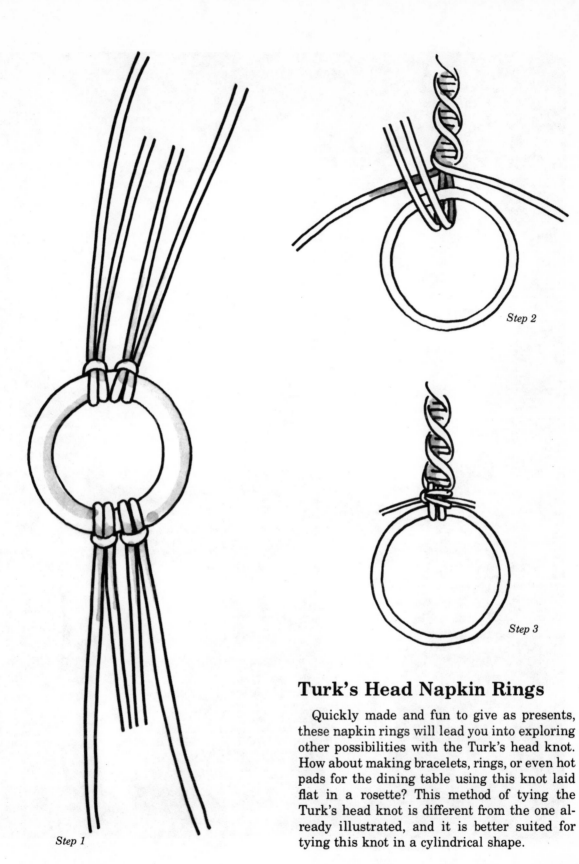

Step 2

Step 3

Step 1

Turk's Head Napkin Rings

Quickly made and fun to give as presents, these napkin rings will lead you into exploring other possibilities with the Turk's head knot. How about making bracelets, rings, or even hot pads for the dining table using this knot laid flat in a rosette? This method of tying the Turk's head knot is different from the one already illustrated, and it is better suited for tying this knot in a cylindrical shape.

Turk's Head Napkin Rings.

Materials

3 yards of 3-ply, #72 dyed cotton seine twine
or any smooth cord, such as nylon or rayon,
for each napkin ring

1 cardboard cylinder, with approximately 1½-
inch diameter, for shaping

White glue

NOTE: Every turn or loop in this knot is called a
"bight." The Turk's Head Knot can be
made with 3, 5, or more bights.

Step 1

Measure and cut one 3-yard length of cord for
each napkin ring. The ends are easier to work
with if you wrap a small piece of masking tape
around each, flattening it to form a stiff,
pointed shape to thread through the loops of
the knot as it is tied. Start by wrapping the
cord around the cardboard cylinder with end 1
3 to 4 inches long. This leaves about 2½ yards
to be threaded through the knot.

Step 2

Make 2 parallel round turns over the cylinder. These turns produce 3 parallel cords on the
cylinder.

Step 3

Hold cord 1 *over* cord 2 to form a loop, and
then thread cord 3 *over* cord 1 and *under* cord 2.
Pull the entire length of cord 3 through the
loop completely until the knot is finished.

Step 4

Now pull cord 3 *over* cord 1 and *under* cord 2
again. Pull the length through completely as
before.

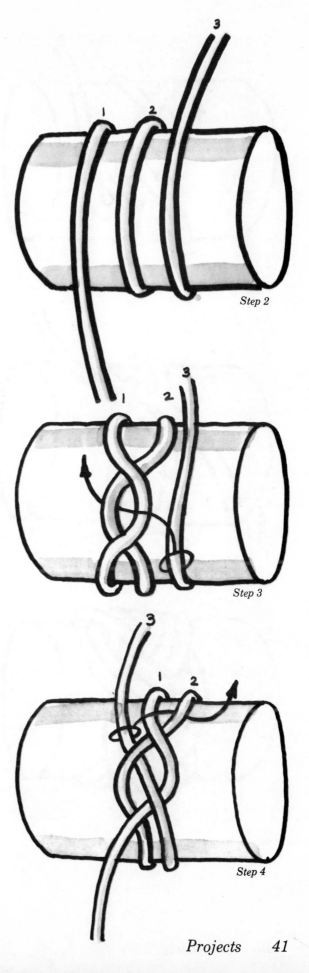

Step 2

Step 3

Step 4

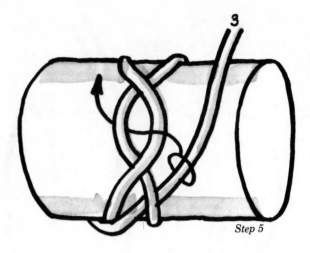

Step 5

Step 6

Step 5

Turn the cylinder over so that the back portion is up. Make another loop, as before, lying the left cord *over* the right cord and bringing cord 3 *over* the first and *under* the second.

Step 6

The two end cords are now in alignment. Weave the long end (cord 3) in and out, keeping it next to cord 1 *at all times*. Continue weaving this cord around the cylinder until you have 3 cords side by side on the entire ring. Carefully remove the ring from the cylinder and glue the cords down to the inside. When the glue is dry, cut off the ends.

Linen Watchband

This watchband wears almost forever, and it's cool in the summertime. It is sized for a woman's wrist. To make it for a man, add ½ inch to the finished measurement of each side.

Materials

22 yards of 3-ply, #12 raw or waxed natural
    linen.
1½-inch buckle
Watch face
White glue

Step 1

Cut 7 lengths of cord, each 3 yards long. Use one length as a holding cord; pin the middle of this cord to a board. Attach the other 6 cords, doubled, with the lark's head knot. This gives you 14 cords, each 1½ yards long. Put a pin in the center of the holding cord, with 3 lark's head knots on each side. Number the cords from left to right.

Step 2

Tie a square knot with the 4 center cords, numbered 6 through 9. Divide the cords of the square knot in half. Tie another square knot using cords 4 through 7 and still another using cords 8 through 11.

Step 3

Divide the cords again. Using the 4 center cords, numbered 6 through 9, tie a square knot.

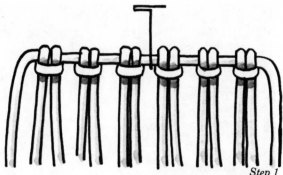

Step 1

Tie a square knot using cords 2 through 5 and another using cords 10 through 13. Your watchband now looks like the illustration.

Step 4
Continue this alternating square knot pattern for 3½ inches. Make the square knots on each side with 3 instead of 4 cords.

Step 5
When you are ready to add the watch, knot the 6 center cords around the bars on either side of the watch face with double half hitches. (see illustration) Continue the alternating square knot pattern, working the center cords back into it, down behind the watch face. When you reach the second bar, knot the 6 center cords onto it as you did for the first bar. Continue the pattern for 2½ more inches. Knot the band onto the buckle with the double half hitch. Bring the ends around to the back. Glue the ends, and when dry, cut them off.

Sampler

You can learn all of the basic knots and create a small wall hanging at the same time by making this sampler. Here it is knotted onto bamboo skewers, which are used as horizontal bars, but you can use any number of other materials (dowels, plexiglas, rods, twigs, etc.).

Materials
112 feet of any hard #21 twisted cord (jute, cotton, or nylon)
8 small bamboo skewers, each 7 inches long
1 metal or plastic ring, 3-inch diameter
White glue

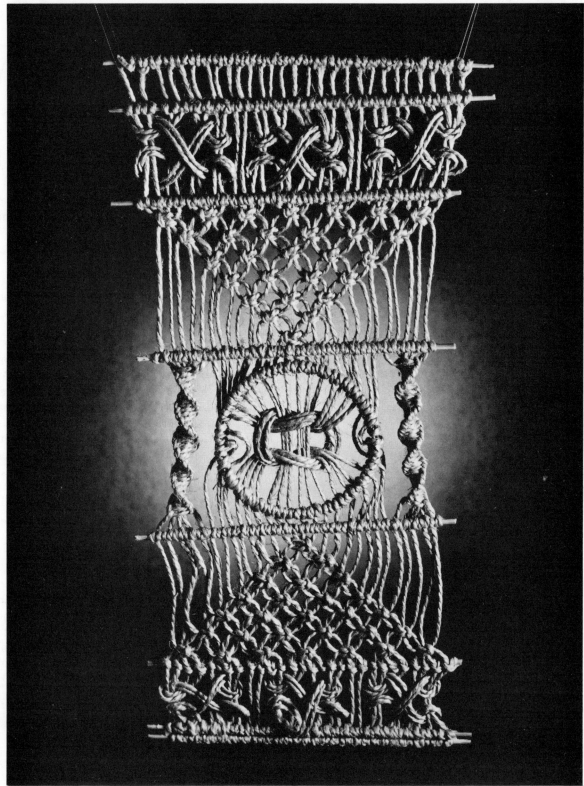

Sampler Project.

Step 1

Cut 14 cords, each 8 feet long. Double each cord and attach it to the first bamboo bar with a lark's head knot. Secure the bar to a board horizontally after knotting on the cords.

Step 2

Drop down ½ inch and knot all of the cords onto the second bar with the double half hitch. Be sure you keep the second bar parallel to the first bar and keep an even amount of space at each end of the bar. Number the cords from left to right.

Step 3

Drop down 1½ inches and knot cords 1 and 2, 7 through 12, 17 through 22, and 27 through 28 onto a third bar with the double half hitch. * Loop cords 3 and 4 around *loosely* to the back of cords 1 and 2. Loop cords 5 and 6 around cords 7 and 8 the same way. Now cross cords 3 and 4 *over* cords 5 and 6. Loop cords 3 and 4 around cords 7 and 8 and cords 5 and 6 around cords 1 and 2. Repeat from * for the rest of the cords, leaving out cords 9 and 10 and 19 and 20. Knot *all* cords onto bar 3 with the double half hitch. Your sampler will look like the illustration if you have looped your cords loosely enough.

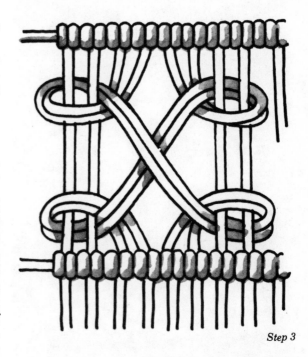

Step 3

Step 4

Beginning at the left, make a row of 7 square knots with 4 cords in each. * Drop the 2 left-hand and 2 right-hand cords. Using 2 cords from each knot in the preceding row, make a row of 6 square knots. Leave about ¼ inch between rows. Repeat from *, dropping 2 cords from each side with every row to form a triangle shape. When you have reached the point, add bar 4 with a double half hitch, carefully keeping it parallel to the bars above (see illustration).

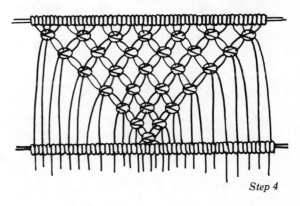

Step 4

Step 5

Using cords 1 through 5, make a 3-inch sinnet of half knots. (There are 3 filler cords.) Repeat with cords 24 through 28.

Step 6

Use cords 14 and 15 to attach the ring just below bar 4. Work down to the left and right with the remainder of the cords, tying them on with double half hitches. * Leave a small loop in cord 6 and knot it back onto the ring. Leave a larger loop in cord 7 and knot it back onto the ring. Repeat from * with cords 22 and 23 (see Tying onto a Ring, page 31).

Step 7

Take the rest of the cords (cords 8 through 21) and tie a large, *loose* square knot in the middle of the ring, using 4 cords from each side to tie around the 6 filler cords. Double half hitch them all back onto the ring in the same order they began.

Step 8

Knot all of the cords onto bar 5, using the double half hitch. Keep the bar parallel to the above bars.

Step 9

Make a square knot with the 4 center cords. Divide the cords in half and drop down ¼ inch. * Make a row of 2 square knots, using 2 more cords from each side. Repeat from *, dividing the cords from each knot and using 2 more cords from each side for each row. When you have reached the last row of 7 square knots, knot all cords onto bar 6 with the double half hitch.

Step 10

Repeat Step 3 for bar 7.

Step 11

Knot onto bar 8 with the double half hitch. Bring the cords around to the back, glue, wait until dry, then cut.

Bell Planter

If you're past the beginner's phase of knotting and want to try your wings a bit, this massive planter is simpler than it looks. And it creates a sensation on the terrace, where the bells chime with every breeze!

Bell Planter.

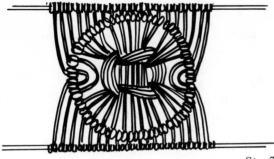

Step 7

Materials

109 yards of 3-ply, #10 natural jute
  1 metal ring, 2-inch diameter
White glue
  2 bamboo poles or wooden dowels, 1-inch diameter
  5 bells
  1 pot, 12- to 14-inch diameter

Step 1

Cut 2 cords, each 2 yards long. Then cut 2 cords, each 5 yards long. Gather all cords at one end with the long cords outside the shorter cords. Secure the cords to a clipboard or another working surface. Move down 16 inches and make a sinnet of half knots by tying the longer cords around the shorter cords. Stop when you are 16 inches from the ends. Slip the ring onto the sinnet. Attach both ends of the sinnet 2 inches from each end of a dowel with double half hitches. Glue under the knots to keep the cords from slipping off of the dowel. Gather each cord group together: Cut two 1½-foot cords and use them to tie a wrap around each cord group, looping each wrapping cord through a bell as you are wrapping. Cut off the ends of the tassel evenly and unravel the cords. At this point you can remove the knotting from your clipboard and attach it by the ring to a hook in your ceiling, to the top of a door, or to any convenient holder high enough to allow you working room.

Step 2

Cut 4 cords, each 3 yards long. Cut 8 cords, each 10 yards long. Attach them to the dowel with lark's head knots. Number them from left to right. Starting from the left, double over 2 of

Step 1

the 3-yard cords. Adjust these cords so that cord 1 is 2 yards long, cords 2 and 3 are each 1 yard long, and cord 4 is 2 yards long. Then double over and attach the eight 10-yard cords so that cords 5, 8, 9, 12, 13, 16, 17, and 20 are each 6 yards long and cords 6, 7, 10, 11, 14, 15, 18, and 19 are each 4 yards long. Double over and attach the remaining two 3-yard cords so that cords 21 and 24 are each 2 yards long and cords 22 and 23 are each 1 yard long. This gives you 24 working cords on the dowel.

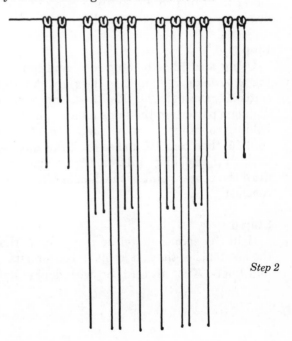

Step 2

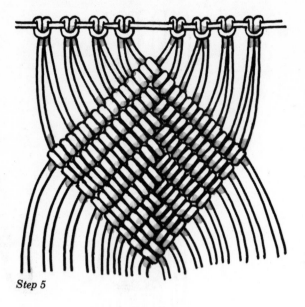

Step 5

hitches. Glue the half knot sinnets to 2 inches from each end of the bar.

Step 7

Gather cords 1 through 4 under the dowel and secure them with a wrap tied from a 1½-foot scrap cord. Add a bell to wrap cord as in Step 1. Cut the tassel cords off evenly and unravel them. Repeat this step for cords 20 through 24.

Step 8

Separate the remaining cords into 4 groups of 4 cords each. Using the first group, tie a half knot sinnet 16 inches long. Be sure your tying cords are the longest in the group. Repeat this for the remaining groups. Tie from the right for the two left-hand groups and from the left for the two right-hand groups.

Step 9

Make the cradle for the pot as follows: Drop down 6 inches and tie a square knot by combining 2 cords from one sinnet with 2 cords from an adjacent sinnet. Use 2 working cords and 2 core cords. Repeat this for the remaining cord groups. Again, divide the cord groups and drop down 4 inches to make another set of square knots. Drop down 4 inches and gather all cords with a 3-inch wrap from a scrap cord. Cut the tassel to any desired length and unravel the ends.

Step 10

Cut a 1-yard cord, double it, and attach it to a bell with a lark's head knot. Tie a 4-inch sinnet of alternating overhand knots. Secure the sinnet to the top ring with a square knot. Glue and cut the ends.

Doorbell Hanging

A good intermediate-skill project, this doorbell hanging is a surefire winner for Christmas gift-giving when knotted in red, green, and silver. It is designed to give you skills in working with color, both in the half hitch and square knot. Scrap ends are used on the ring sides.

Step 3

Make a half knot sinnet 11 inches long by tying the two longer cords around the shorter cords. Repeat for cords 21 through 24. Roll up the ends of cords 5 through 20 and secure them with rubber bands.

Step 4

Using cord 13 as a holding cord, drop down 3 inches and tie on cord 12 with a double half hitch. Remember that the holding cord stays on *top* of the tying cord. Continue tying at a 45-degree angle cords 11 through 5.

Step 5

Using cord 12 as holding cord, and continuing at a 45-degree angle to the right, knot on cords 14 through 20. Tie the remainder of diamond pattern in the same manner, using as holding cords first cord 14, then cord 11, then cord 15, then cord 10, and so on. Take care not to tie in the holding cord from the previous row until the center point of the diamond has been reached.

Step 6

Hold the second dowel horizontally so that the bar touches the last knots in the sinnets of half knots. Knot all cords on with double half

Doorbell Hangings.

Step 2

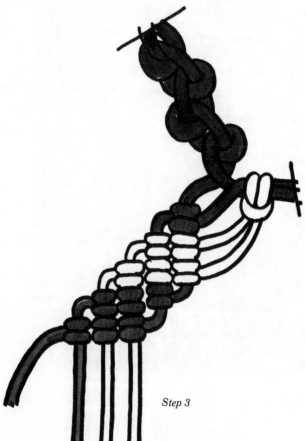

Step 3

Materials

20 yards of 3-ply #21 dyed or plain cotton seine twine or silk rattail in *each* of 2 colors

20 feet of #21 cotton seine twine, silk rattail, or any other scraps available in a contrasting third color.

1 wooden curtain ring, 2¼-inch inside diameter

1 #22 brass harness bell or equivalent

Step 1

Cut two 2-yard lengths of the first color of cotton seine twine. Secure the centers to a clipboard or pin them onto a bar 2 inches from the center point. Using these cords, make a 3-inch sinnet of alternating overhand knots.

Step 2

Cut two 2½-yard lengths of the second color. Form the sinnet into a loop and drop the 2 outside cords. Double the 2 second-color cords, and using the 2 inside cords of the sinnet (see illustration), add the doubled cords with the lark's head knot. Pull the two holding cords taut.

Step 3

Before beginning the first section of the doorbell hanging, number the cords from left to right, 1 through 8. Use cord 1 as a holding cord. Knot cords 2 through 4 onto cord 1 with the double half hitch, holding it down toward the center at a 45-degree angle. Next use cord 2 as a holding cord and repeat. Next use cord 3 and repeat. Leave cord 3 hanging; do not knot it into the next row (see illustration). Knot in cord 4 and leave it hanging also. Knot in cord 1 again (just one knot) and leave it hanging also. The work now looks like the illustration. Bring cord 2 around in front of the cords. Using cord 2 as holding cord, knot the other cords (1, 4, 3) onto it as before. Repeat using cords 1, 4, and 3 as holding cords. Now bring both outside cords, left and right, together loosely to form a double holding cord. Knot all the other cords onto the double holding cord. Pull the holding cord tight from both sides.

Step 4

Your project now looks like the illustration. Position the bell in front of the center 4 cords, and using the bell as holding cord, knot all 4 cords onto it with the double half hitch. Then knot all cords onto the wooden curtain ring with the double half hitch. Pull the cords taut and adjust so that the bell hangs in the center of the ring. Glue all cords to the back of the ring and cut them off.

Step 5

Cut 20 cords, each 1 foot long, from the third color. Fold the cords in half and tie them onto the ring with lark's head knots, starting near the top of the ring and continuing around both sides until about a 2-inch space remains at the bottom of the ring.

Step 6

Cut 6 cords, each 3 yards long, of one color used in the top section and 4 cords, each 3 yards long, of the other color. Double the cords and use lark's head knots to add them to the open space at the bottom of the ring. Position the cords so that the darker of the two colors is on the outside, both right and left, and the lighter color is in the middle.

Step 7

Make a pattern of alternating square knots. Start the square knot pattern from each side. Continue for 6 inches, bringing the pattern to a point in the center.

Step 8

Gather all cords and tie a 2-inch sinnet of square knots around all center cords with 2 cords from each side. Cut a tassel to the desired length and unravel the cords.

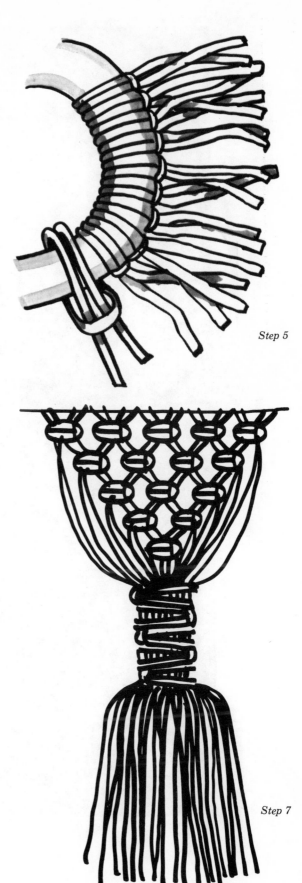

Step 5

Step 7

Blue Plant Hanger.

Blue Plant Hanger

Materials

153 yards of 3-ply, #72 cotton white line, dyed
  blue
Metal ring, 2-inch diameter
Wooden or metal hoop, 6-inch diameter

Step 1

Cut 16 cords, each 3½ yards long. Cut one
2-yard length and tie a sinnet of square knots
over a 5-inch length of the 3½-yard cords, starting 2½ inches from the center point of the 3½
yard cords, and continuing 2½ inches past the
center. Use a clipboard to hold the cords 2½
inches from the center point. Fold the sinnet in
half and slip it through the 2-inch metal ring.

Step 2

Cut a 1½-yard cord and tie a 2-inch wrap
over all the cords. Pull the wrap cord tight and
cut off the 4 short ends (see illustration).

Step 3

Separate the cords into 4 groups of 8 cords
each and tie 5 crown knots (see illustration).

Step 4

Attach the cords to the hoop in groups of 8
with the double half hitch. Leave 3 to 4 inches
of space between the end of the crown knot sinnet and hoop. Adjust the groups of knots so that
the hoop hangs evenly.

Step 3

Step 5

Cut 4 cords, each 1 yard long. Tie a 1-inch
wrap around the ends of each cord group. Unravel the ends, if desired (see illustration).

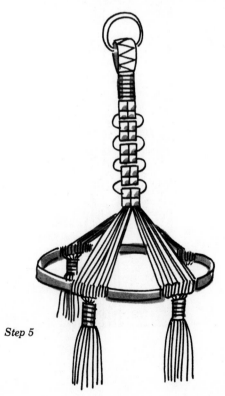

Step 5

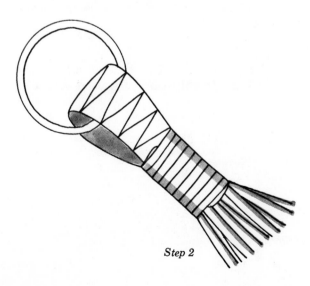

Step 2

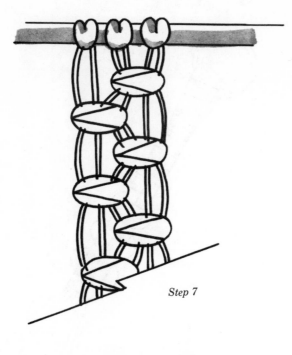

Step 7

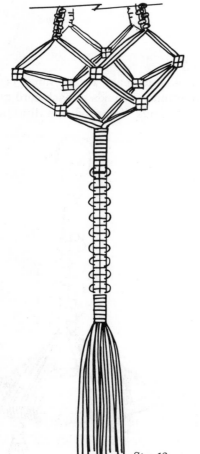

Step 12

Step 6

Cut 12 cords, each 8 yards long. Separate the cords into 4 groups of 3 each, fold them in half, and attach each onto the hoop with a lark's head knot.

Step 7

* Using the 4 right-hand cords, make a square knot. Drop the 2 right-hand cords. Using the 4 left-hand cords, make a square knot. Drop the 2 left-hand cords. Repeat the pattern from * for 18 inches. Then repeat for the 3 remaining groups of cords (see illustration).

Step 8

Make the cradle as follows: Separate the cords into groups of 3 each. Drop down 6 inches and tie* one row of crown knots, using half the cords from each group for each. Separate the cords again. Drop down 4 inches and repeat from *.

Step 9

Cut one 1-yard cord. Beginning 2 inches below the last row of crown knots, tie a 3-inch wrap around all of the cords.

Step 10

Separate the cords into 4 groups of 6 cords each. Tie crown knots for 8 inches.

Step 11

Cut one 1-yard cord. Tie a 2-inch wrap around all cords immediately below the crown knots.

Step 12

Drop down 18 inches and cut all cords. Unravel the tassel (see illustration for Step 5).

Mini Hammock Tote Bag (see following page).

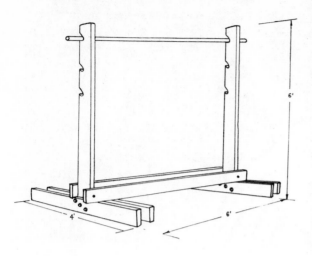

Mini Hammock Tote Bag

When you complete this tote bag, you'll have all the knowledge necessary to make a hammock! The process is identical; only the size is different. You may find that hammock making is easier with a special frame to hold and support your knotting. Here is an illustration of the one I designed and constructed. It's very simple to assemble and requires only 4 six-foot and 2 eight-foot lengths of 2-inch by 6-inch boards, 6 bolts, and 8 screws, plus a 7 foot pole to fit across the top to hold your knotting. I have found myself using it for countless projects, small and large, because the bar can be adjusted from a sitting to a standing working height.

Materials

112 yards or 2 balls of 5-ply, 5 millimeter bleached jute

2 metal rings, 4-inch diameter

2 wooden dowels with finials, 14-inch lengths

White glue

Step 1

Cut 2 cords, each 7 feet long, and cover both rings with vertical lark's head knots, leaving a 3-inch space open.

Step 2

Cut 20 cords, each 4 feet long. Double each cord and attach half of the cords to each metal ring, covering the ends of the cords used to cover the ring.

Step 3

To make the clews, take the 2 left-hand cords and * weave them to the right through the rest of the cords. Attach them to the right-hand end of the wooden dowel with a double half hitch. Take the first 2 right-hand cords and repeat from *, weaving to the left and attaching the cords to the left-hand end of the dowel. Take the next 2 left-hand cords and repeat this sequence from each side until the last cords have been woven. Tie the last 2 cords together at the point of the weaving with an overhand knot and attach them to the dowel.

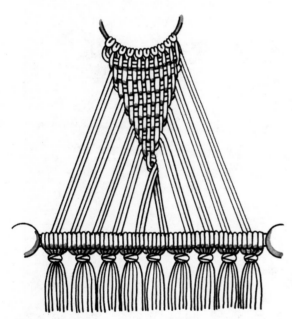

Step 4

NOTE: This is exactly the way clews for a hammock are made, except that the ring is not covered with cord and the wooden stretcher bars have holes drilled for the cords to go through instead of around them.

Step 4

Cut 36 cords, each 2 yards long. Divide the cords into 9 groups of four. Loop each group over the first dowel from the inside between the double half hitches of the clew cords. Tie a 1-inch scrap cord around the ends of each group, forming tassels. Tie tassels with square knots. Include the ends of the adjacent clew cords (see illustration).

Step 5

* Drop down 1 to 1½ inches and tie a row of overhand knots, using 2 cords for each. Divide the cords, and repeat from *. Continue for 30 inches or until you have 8 inches of cords left.

Step 6

Attach the cords to the second dowel, as described in step 4. Cut all tassels to 4-inch lengths. Dab a bit of glue on each square knot to secure it.

Step 7

To close the sides, cut 2 cords, each 1 yard long. Use 1 cord for each side (see illustration). Starting at the bottom of the bag, loop the cord around each bag's side cords and then tie an overhand knot with it. Bring the cord together in the center of the side and tie another overhand knot. Then bring the cord around the side cords again until you reach the top. Stop with the last side knots. Glue and cut the cords.

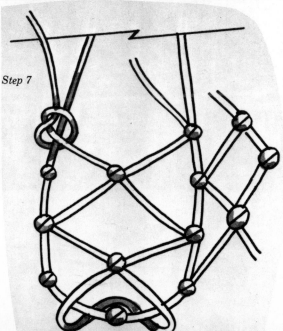

Step 7

Hoop Hanging

Reminiscent of the Southwest, this small wall hanging may be enlarged to any scale you wish by enlarging the size of the beads, rope, wooden ring, and feathers to meet the diameter of your hoop. This project is knotted almost entirely with vertical lark's head knots.

Materials

20 yards of #21 rust cotton seine twine
 1 hoop (preferably wooden), 7-inch diameter
32 wooden beads, ⅜-inch diameter
12 yards of 5-ply, 5 millimeter natural raw linen or jute
 1 wooden curtain ring, 2¼-inch diameter
 1 dozen rooster feathers (approximately) in any mixture of brown, tan, black, or white colors
White glue

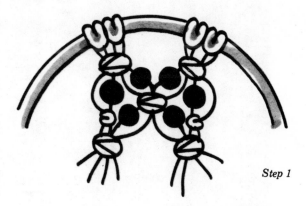

Step 1

Step 1

Cut 4 cords, each 4 yards long, of rust cotton seine twine. Double over the cords and mount them onto the top of the larger hoop with lark's head knots. Separate the cords into 2 groups of 4 each. Tie 1 square knot with each group. Number the cords from left to right. String beads on cords 4 and 5. Using the beaded cords as fillers, tie a center square knot around them below the beads with cords 3 and 6. String beads on cords 2 and 7. Tie a vertical lark's head knot below each bead with cords 1 and 6. String beads on cords 3 and 6. Bring the cords back into their original groups 1 through 4 and 5 through 8 and tie a square knot with each (see illustration).

Hoop Hanging.

Step 2

Cut 4 cords, each 3 yards long, of natural raw linen. Double over the cords and mount them onto the hoop (2 cords on each side) with lark's head knots. Make an alternating vertical lark's head braid for 1½ inches (see illustration).

Step 3

Continue with the cotton twine. Using cord 2 as a holding cord, tie 5 vertical lark's head knots with cord 1. Repeat this using cord 7 as the holding cord and cord 8 as the tying cord.

Step 4

String beads on cords 3 and 6. Use the beaded cords to tie a square knot around cords 4 and 5. Cut 2 cords, each 2 yards long, of cotton twine. Double over the cords and mount one each to cords 3 and 6 with lark's head knots.

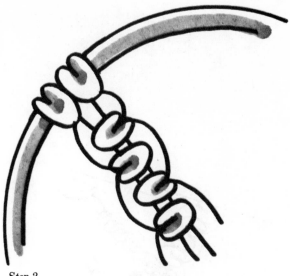

Step 2

Step 5

At this point, renumber the cotton cords from left to right, 1 through 12. Using cords 4 and 5 as fillers, tie a square knot with cords 3 through 6. Repeat with cords 7 through 10. Divide the cords of the square knots, and string beads on cords 5 and 8. Using cords 6 and 7 as fillers, tie a square knot around them with cords 5 and 8. Using cord 4 as a holding cord, tie 2 vertical lark's head knots with cord 3. Repeat this, using cord 10 to tie around cord 9.

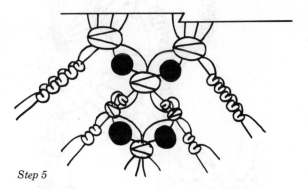

Step 5

Step 6

* Use the 4 left-hand linen cords as holding cords. Letter them from left to right, A through H. Tie cotton cords 1 and 2 onto them one by one with double half hitches. String beads on cords A and D. Then tie cords 3 and 4 onto A through D with the double half hitch (see the illustration for step 9).

Step 7

Tie cords A through D onto the small wooden ring with vertical lark's head knots. Repeat from * for the right-hand linen cords, E through H. Using cord 2 as holding cord, tie 9 vertical lark's head knots with cord 1. Using cord 4 as a holding cord, tie 4 vertical lark's head knots with cord 3. Using cord 3 as holding cord, tie a row of double half hitches with cords 1 and 2. Using cord 4 as holding cord, tie another row of the double half hitch, using cords 1, 2, 3 as tying cords. Tie cords 1 and 2 onto the ring with the vertical lark's head knot. Gather cords 1 through 4 together, and using the longest cord as a tying cord, tie a ½-inch wrap around the other 3 cords. Cut the tassel 1 foot long and unravel the cords (see illustration for Step 9).

Step 8

Gather the linen cords into 2 groups in *back* of the ring. Bring the cotton cords over the *front* of the ring. Pull the cotton cords straight down and tie them to the bottom of the ring with the double half hitch. Bring group E through H around and to the front of the cotton cords. Then * double half hitch the cords individually onto the ring. Bring group A through D around and to the front of *both* groups of cords. Repeat from *. The wooden center ring now looks like the illustration in Step 9.

Step 9

Bring the two groups of linen cords down in the same order as they started, with an alternating vertical lark's head braid, until the braid is long enough to reach the outer ring. Tie the cords onto the ring with the double half hitch. Tie 2 overhand knots under each group. Cut the resulting tassels to 4-inch lengths and unravel the ends. Cut the remaining cotton center cords to 19-inch lengths and scatter the remaining beads on them at random intervals, tying an overhand knot below each bead to place it. Stick the quills at the end of each feather through spaces in the sinnet of 9 lark's head knots on each side. Secure at the back with a drop of glue.

Spiral Dog Leash

This project gives you practice in tying long sinnets of cords, particularly the alternate method for square knot.

Materials
50 feet of ⅛-inch, #24 nylon
1 brass snaffle hook
White glue
Large crochet hooks

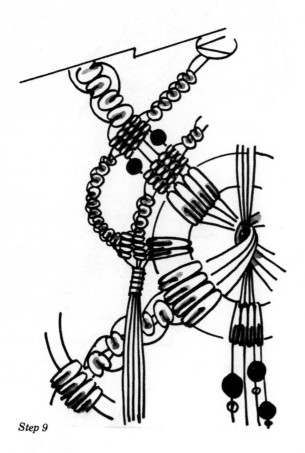

Step 9

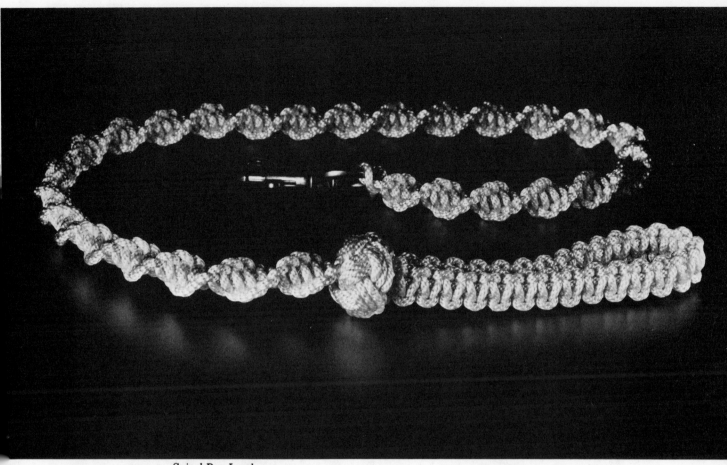

Spiral Dog Leash.

Step 1

Cut 2 cords, each 25 feet long. Fuse the ends (see What to Do with Ends, page 00). Attach the cords to the ring with lark's head knots, so that you have 4 cords. Adjust the cords so that the outside ones are 19 feet long and the inside ones are 6 feet long. Make a 3-inch spiral sinnet of half knots.

Step 2

Continue the sinnet with square knots for 1 foot.

Step 3

Leave 1 long end and cut the others to 6 inches in length. Fuse the ends. Using a large crochet hook, interweave the 3 short ends into the area where the half knots and square knots meet. Glue and cut the ends. Fuse and remove glue.

Step 4

Using the long end, tie a Turk's head knot around both sinnets where they meet.

NOTE: To make the Turk's head knot, refer to the Turk's head napkin rings project (see page 39). If it is easier for you, take a cardboard cylinder and place it over the junction on the dog leash where your knot is to be placed. Then continue as shown for Turk's head napkin rings. When the knot is tied loosely, remove the cylinder and tighten the knot, beginning with the end that is attached to the leash. Continue around the knot, pulling the same cord, until the knot is completely taut. Glue and cut the ends.

Fancy Pants Belt.

Fancy Pants Belt

Made very much the same as a sampler, this knotted belt will be a source of pleasure for years. It is suitable for a woman or a man.

Materials
128 yards of #12 raw linen or #12 cable laid flax
1 1½-inch brass buckle
White glue

Step 1
Cut 8 cords, each 16 yards long. Double them over and roll up the ends, starting from 2 feet below the midpoint and rolling down toward each end. Secure with rubber bands.

Step 2
Pin 2 doubled cords down to a board. Make a square knot, using all 4 cords. This forms the doubled point. Divide the cords and add 1 doubled cord on each side with the square knot. Pin each of the 3 knots in place. Add the rest of the cords in the same manner, knotting a solid alternating square knot pattern as you go (see illustration).

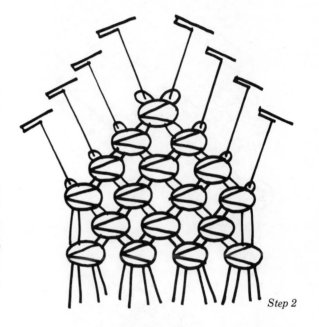

Step 2

Step 3
When you have added all the cords, continue the same pattern for 4 inches.

Step 4
Make four 1-inch sinnets of square knots.

Step 5
Divide the cords in half. Drop 2 cords on each side. Tie three ½-inch sinnets of square knots across. Tie a sinnet of 4 vertical lark's head knots with both sets of side cords, using the outside cord to tie around the inner.

Step 6
Tie four ½-inch sinnets of square knots (see illustration).

Step 7
Repeat Step 5.

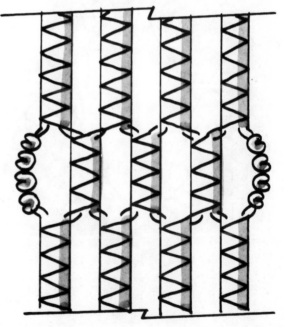

Step 6

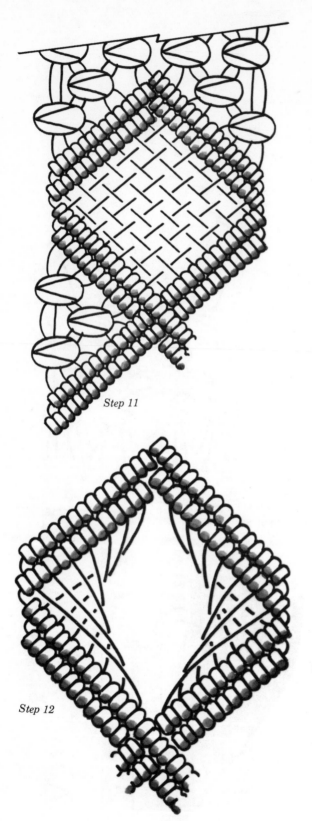

Step 11

Step 12

Step 8
Repeat Step 4.

Step 9
Tie an alternating square knot pattern for 1 inch. Stop on a row with 4 knots across. Number the cords from left to right.

Step 10 (First Diamond)
Using cord 8 as a holding cord, tie on cords 9 and 10 with the double half hitch. Make a square knot with cords 11 through 14 and then hitch 11 and 12 onto cord 8. Make a square knot with cords 13 and 16 and then double half hitch them onto cord 8. Repeat for the right side, using cord 9 as a holding cord. Knot another row of double half hitches immediately under, using cords 7 and 10 as holding cords. When you have finished the rows, hitch holding cord 8 onto the row below, and do the same with holding cord 9.

Step 11
Weave all center cords together, over and under. Using cords 7, 10, 8, and 9 as holding cords, double half hitch the center cords to double rows, forming a diamond shape (see illustration). This pattern of double half hitched rows is used for the entire length of the belt with different patterns inside each diamond. Fill in one each side between the diamond patterns with an alternating square knot pattern. (See illustration).

Step 12 (Second Diamond)
When all cords are knotted onto the upper set of double bars for this pattern, and hanging loosely, take the cord nearest the upper point and bring it down. Hitch it onto the far left-hand side of the lower double bars. Repeat this, hitching the next cord to the left onto the right of the first cord. Continue the pattern (see illustration).

Step 13 (Third Diamond)
Make 7 sinnets of alternating overhand knots to fit inside this diamond.

Step 14 (Fourth Diamond)

Using 2 cords from each corner, tie a loose square knot around all other cords in this diamond.

Step 15

Repeat Step 12.

Step 16

Repeat Step 14.

Step 17

Repeat Step 13.

Step 18

Repeat Step 12.

Step 19

Repeat Step 14.

Step 20

Repeat Step 11.

Step 21

Working from the sides down to the middle, tie an alternating square knot pattern for 1 inch past the point of the last diamond.

Step 22

Repeat Step 4 through Step 8.

Step 23

Tie an alternating square knot pattern for 4½ inches (for a 38-inch belt) or longer if needed.

Step 24

Hitch all cords onto the center post of the buckle. Glue and cut the ends.

Step 25

Cut 2 scrap cords, each 2 feet long. Double over and use the 4 cords to tie a 3-inch sinnet of square knots. Wrap the sinnet around the belt 2 inches from the buckle. Tie the ends together, also weaving the ends into the belt as you go, securing the loop to the belt. Glue and cut the ends.

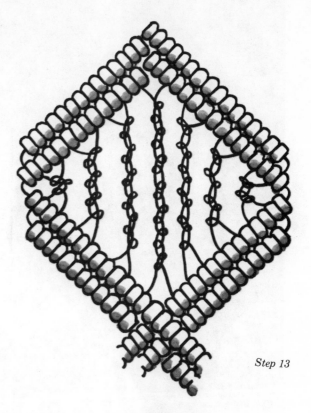

Step 13

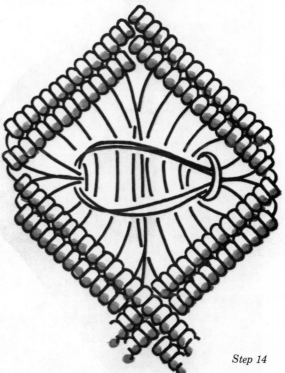

Step 14

"Seeing Double" Plant Hanger.

"Seeing Double" Plant Hanger

You'd better have a stout hook when you hang this plant hanger, it's heavy! The crown knot sinnet at the top is 5 inches in diameter. You can get lots of practice in handling large numbers of cords with this project, and also learn to knot the berry pattern, a three dimensional shape that you'll use in many other ways. This berry pattern is knotted using 6 cords; usually it is made using 8. You can do it either way.

Materials
320 yards of natural jute
one 4-inch steel ring (don't substitute wood or bamboo)
White glue

Step 1
Cut thirty-two 30-foot lengths of jute and double them through a 4-inch steel ring. You'll have sixty-four 15 foot lengths of cord on the ring. Separate the cords into 4 groups of 16 cords each, and tie a large overhand knot near the end of each group, using all the cords in the group. This will keep them organized while you do the next step.

Step 2
Tie a 10-inch sinnet of crown knots using all 4 cord groups, taking care to pull all cords taut *individually* after tying each crown knot.

Step 3
Separate each group in half, after untying the overhand knot in each. You'll now have 8 groups of 8 cords each. * Using one of the cords, tie a sinnet of vertical half hitches around the other seven cords in its group, letting the knots twist as they are tied. Continue for 14 inches. Tuck the ends of the tying cords under your last half hitches, glue, and cut. See illustration.

Step 4
Cut off one cord from each group at the bottom of each sinnet, and save. Divide each group in half; you'll have 3 cords in each. Drop down 4 inches, and with each group of 3, make a square knot, using one cord as a core. Using any two

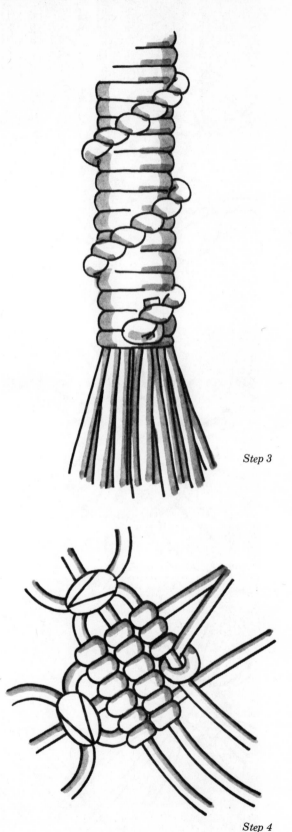

Step 3

Step 4

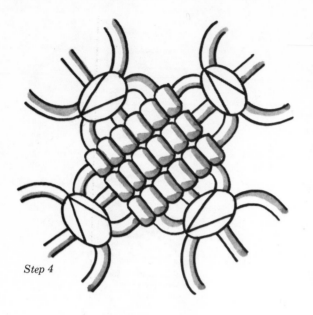

Step 4

adjacent groups, knot a berry pattern directly underneath the square knots. See illustration. Tie 2 square knots under each berry, using 3 cords for each knot. See illustration. Pull the square knots tight and push out the knot from the back. It will curve into a semicircular shape. See illustration.

Step 5

Using the same cord groupings—weave adjacent groups together. See illustration. When they are all woven together, hold all cords 6 inches below the berry knots and tie a temporary scrap cord around all. Separate cords into 4 groups of 12 cords each. Tie a sinnet of 6 crown knots. Untie the scrap cord and discard.

Step 6

Repeat Step 3, using one of the reserved cords to tie around each group of 7 cords. Start the sinnet of half hitches as in illustration. Continue for 12 inches. Tuck ends under, glue, and cut.

Step 7

Weave all cord group together as in Step 5. Bring all cords together 6 inches below the last knots in the sinnets of Step 6—and using one of the cords, tie a 4 inch wrap around all cords. Glue and cut end of the wrapping cord. Cut tassel to desired length.

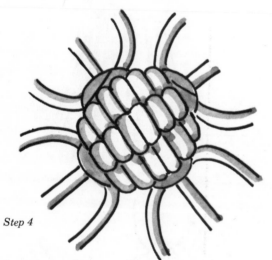

Step 4

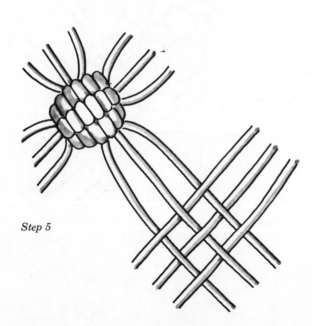

Step 5

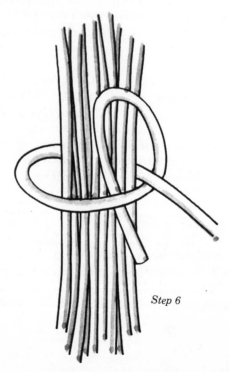

Step 6

6
The Macramé Gallery

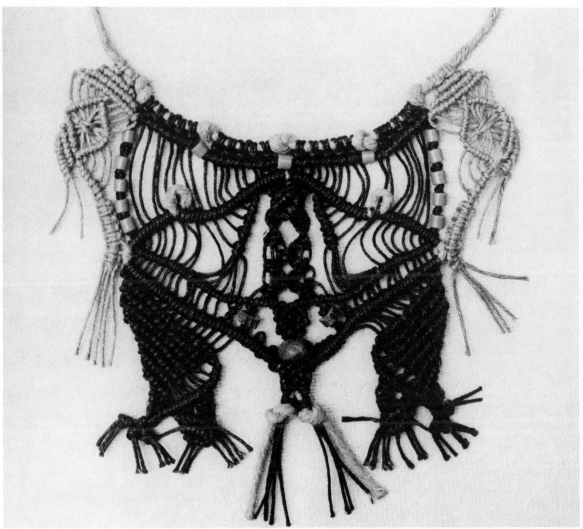

Photo: Rikki Ripp

Neckpiece by Rikki Ripp. Natural and dyed jute with glass and wooden beads. Note how the holding cord has been tied in an overhand knot at intervals and how the dyed cord has been knotted on in-between the overhand knots. Collection of the artist.

Photo: Rikki Ripp

Belt by Rikki Ripp. Look at the pattern on the underneath side. Also look at the way it was begun on the buckle and ended with a short fringe. 2 colors macra-cord. Collection of the artist.

Mask "Mine Medusa" by Mary Ann Zotto-Beltz. Wrapping is used effectively in this sophisticated mask. Goat hair and jute, with guinea fowl feathers interspersed over a clay mask. 20 by 18 by 9 inches. Collection of Edward and Virginia Krictz.

Neckpiece "All in Jest" by Barbara Jurgensen. This piece was done entirely using the horizontal double half hitch with Turk's head button knots added. Linen and jute with glass and wooden beads. Collection of the artist.

Neckpiece "Golden Spoons" by Barbara Jurgensen. The sections on this neckpiece were joined at the bottoms so as not to show fringes. Linen and jute with beads and metal "saltspoons." Collection of the artist.

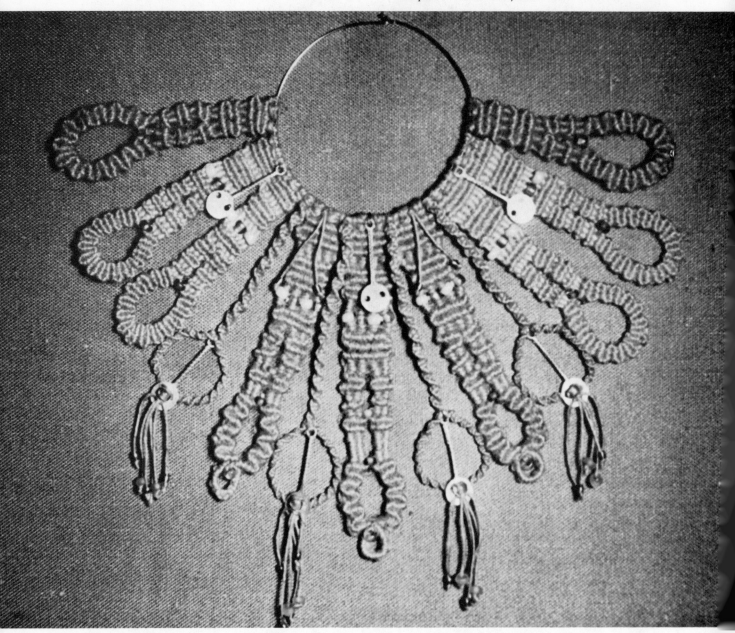

Photo: Ralph Dicks

Sculpture "Double Wings" by Jon B. Wahling. This is a freestanding piece that owes its rigidity to a steel armature and the strength gained from the rows of tightly knotted double half hitches. Jute, wood, and steel. 80 by 40 inches. Collection of the University of Texas Art Museum, Austin, Texas.

Photo: J. Rook

Mirrored wall hanging "Sunburst" by Arlene Pitlick.
Begun on a ring around a center mirror, this wall
hanging was expanded by adding new cords with every
added ring. Welt cord and beads. 30-inch diameter.
Collection of the artist.

Halter by Paul Johnson. Macramé lends itself to opulence, as represented by this lovely halter. The knotting, mostly alternating overhand knots and double half hitches, is almost indistinguishable from the beadwork. Black waxed linen lined in ultrasuede. Hackle feathers and beads with 2 rock crystal formations.

Mirrored wall hanging "Double" by Arlene Pitlick. Notice the interest created by the repetition of a circular pattern with two different materials, rope and glass. Jute and wools. 18 by 60 inches. Collection of Elizabeth Marchand.

Photo: J. Rook

Sculpture "Homage to Maija Grotell" by Jon B. Wahling. Freestanding knotting of sisal, wood, and steel. 68 inches by 28 inches by 24 inches. Collection of Harold Schneider, Columbus, Ohio.

Photo: D. R. Goff—Quicksilver

Headdress by Paul Johnson. Sinnets of alternating overhand knots and double half hitches in black waxed linen hold the beads in this theatrical headdress. Rock crystal, smoke quartz, glass, and crystal beads. Rooster, turkey, and guinea hen feathers.

Wall hanging "Magic Mandalas" by Sara Travis. This piece proves that just about anything is material for the inventive knotter. A combination of weaving and macramé. Wool, feathers, corn shucks, clay, wood, and bone. 18 by 36 inches. Collection of Suzanne Edison, Baltimore.

The Macramé Gallery   77

Detail of below.

Wall mask "Teenage Lust" by Susan Aaron-Taylor. This piece is a marvel of intricate coiled basketry (see detail). Although it is not technically macramé, the similarity of techniques and the look of the finished piece renders it suitable for inclusion in this book. Metallic and synthetic cords. 27 by 14 inches. Collection of the artist.

Photo: Harry William Taylor

Photo: Michael Tull.

Detail of neckpiece by Carolyn Bell. Silk rattail and shells form a beautiful combination in this intricate neckpiece. Note the shaping done with double half hitches. Collection of Arlene Hirschfelder.

Detail of wall sculpture by Carolyn Bell. Weaving with rope is used to advantage in this 4½- by 2-foot wall sculpture. Half hitches are used for shaping the forms. Natural cotton rope. Collection of the artist.

Photo: Michael Tull.

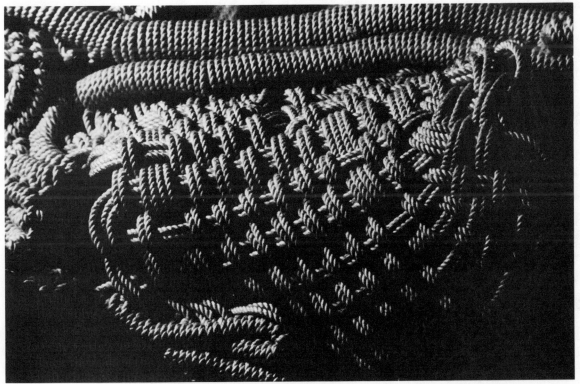

*Sculpture "Out of the Depths" by Mary Ann Zotto-Beltz.
This fiber work hangs from the ceiling and turns slowly
with the air currents to create a constantly changing work
of art for the viewer. Hand-dyed jute with fur and wooden
beads. 5 by 3 by 3½ inches. Collection of Donald and
Betty Oswell.*

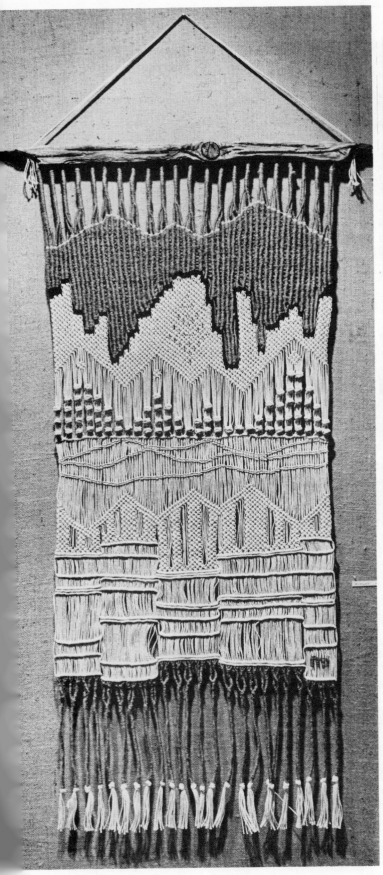

Wall hanging by Alice A. Lassiter. The pheasant feathers make an interesting contrast in texture and color on this hanging. Jute and horsehair. 30 by 66 inches. Collection of the artist.

Wall hanging "Michigan" by Majel Chance Obata. This is a good combination of formal and informal design in the same piece. White cotton and blue wool. 4 feet by 20 inches. Collection of Nori Obata.

*Wall hanging by Pamalee Reève Macon. A beautiful
exercise in the diagonal double half hitch, the reversed
double half hitch, and the overhand knot. Note the
abundance of tassels, which become the major design
element. Natural cotton ropes. 8½ by 10½ feet. Owned by
Maui Intercontinental Hotel, Maui, Hawaii.*

Lamp shade by Sharon Robinson. Note the use of the square knot bobble in this lamp shade. Nylon seine twine over old lamp shade frame. Collection of the artist.

Lamp shade by Sharon Robinson. Nylon seine twine over old lamp shade frame.

Neckpiece by Sharon Robinson. This is an intricate neckpiece (see detail) done completely with the double half hitch. Maroon macra cord with crystal beads. Collection of the artist.

Hairpiece by Alice Wansor. Waxed natural linen and wooden heads.

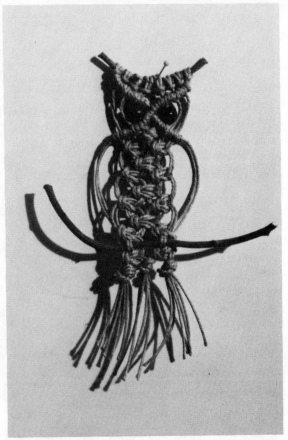

Owl by Alice Wansor. Waxed natural linen and wooden beads.

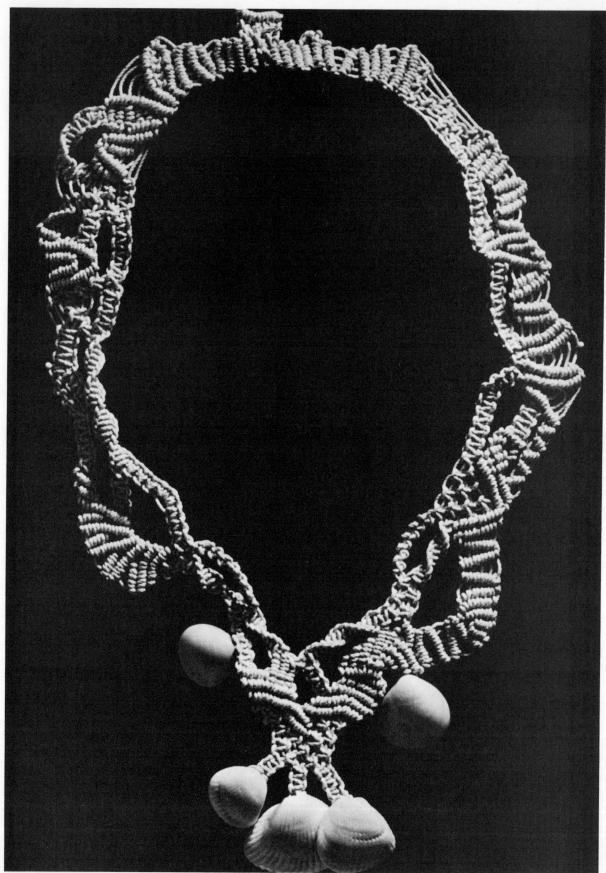

Neckpiece by Carolyn Bell. All square knots and double half hitches, the solidarity of the knotting on this neckpiece is offset by the delicacy of the shells. Collection of Elizabeth Ely Fuller.

Neckpiece by Alice A. Lassiter. Note the use of the vertical double half hitch in the horizontal bonds going across this necklace. They add another variation in texture. Gold and black waxed nylon with ebony and glass beads. Collection of the artist.

Detail of above.

Wall hanging by Nancy Larcomb. This circular hanging is a bold statement. Much of it is wrapped and twisted. Unusual for macramé, the ends have been worked into the knotting so that they don't show. Sisal and unspun wool. 52-inch diameter. Collection of the artist.

Photo: Stefan Findel

Covered bottle by Rikki Ripp. This is an interesting solution to covering a bottle with cord, more involved than most. Instead of beginning at the bottom, as most have done, the craftsman has started at the neck and added cords as the bottle widened. White cotton seine twine. 8 inches high. Collection of the artist.

Photo: Stefan Findel

Key rings by Betsy Milam. Here are three variations on a theme, shaping with the double half hitch. They could be enlarged to form the basis for a wall hanging. Silk soutache, cotton, and linen cords.

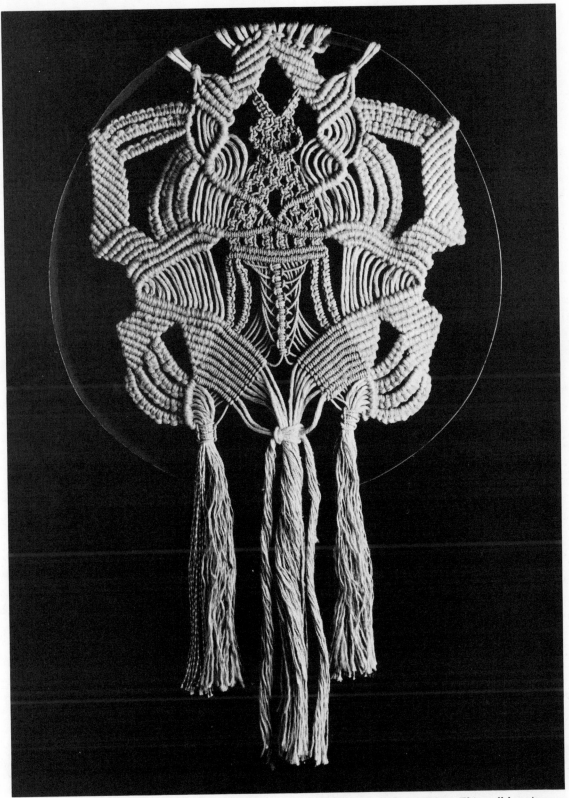

*Wall hanging by Betsy Milam. This wall hanging
puts to use an old barrel hoop. Cords were added as the
knotting progressed to create a rather formal design. 3
shades of brown in cotton seine twine and raw linen.
18-inch diameter. Collection of the artist.*

Photo: Stefan Findel

Vest by Betsy Milam. This vest was knotted over a dressmaker's form, so it is comfortable to wear, and shapes to the body without fasteners. Dyed cotton seine twine and pony beads. Collection of Bucky Milam.

Photo: Stefan Findel

Wall hanging "Toot Your Own Horn" by Betsy
Milam. Note how the color is worked into and
around this hanging. Sometimes it's fun to start knotting
and just let the cord find its own way. Natural jute, white
cotton cord, and a broken trombone. 6 by 4 feet. Collection
of the artist.

The Macramé Gallery   93

Sources and Supplies

Frederick J. Fawcett, Inc.
129 South Street
Boston, Massachusetts 02111

William Condon & Sons, Ltd.
65 Queen Street
Charlottetown, P.O. Box 129
Prince Edward Island, Canada

The Yarn Depot
545 Sutter Street
San Francisco, California 94102

Lily Mills Co.
P.O. Box 88
Shelby, North Carolina 28150

The Niddy Noddy
416 Albany Post Road
Croton-on-Hudson, New York 10520

Greenberg & Hammer, Inc.
24 West 57 Street
New York, New York 10022

P. C. Herwig Co.
Route 2, Box 140
Milaca, Minnesota 56353

Walsall Saddlery
9 Murray Street
New York, New York

AAA Cordage Co., Inc.
3238 N. Clark Street
Chicago, Illinois 60657

Greentree Ranch Woods
Countryside Handweavers
163 N. Carter Lake Road
Loveland, Colorado 80537

Hollywood Fancy Feather
512 S. Broadway
Los Angeles, California 90013

Las Manos, Inc.
12215 Coitrd (in Olla Podrida)
Dallas, Texas 75230

Macramé and Weaving Supply Co.
63 E. Adams #403
Chicago, Illinois 60614

Oregon Handspun Wool
P.O. Box 132
Monroe, Oregon 97456

Bibliography

Anchor Manual of Needlework, 3d. ed. Newton Center, Massachusetts: Wm. Cloves and Sons Ltd., 1968.

Ashley, Clifford W. *The Ashley Book of Knots.* Garden City, New York: Doubleday & Co., 1944.

DeDillmont, Therese. *Encyclopedia of Needlework.* Alsace, France: Mulhouse.

Graumont, Raoul, and Hensel, John. *Encyclopedia of Knots and Fancy Rope Work.* Cambridge, Maryland: Cornell Maritime Press, 1952.

Harvey, Virginia I. *Macramé, the Art of Creative Knotting.* New York: Van Nostrand-Reinhold Co., 1967.

Meilach, Donna Z. *Macramé, Creative Design in Knotting.* New York: Crown Publishers, Inc., 1971.

Phillips, Mary Walker. *Step by Step Macramé.* New York: Golden Press, 1970.

Sylvia's Book of Macramé Lace. Ca. 1882–1885.

Index